A CLEAR VOICE

A CLEAR VOICE

DOUGLAS YOUNG
POET AND POLYMATH

*A Selection from his Writings
with a Memoir*

'Αποθανὼν ἔτι λαλεῖ
—*Hebr. xi, 4*

MACDONALD PUBLISHERS
Loanhead · Midlothian · Scotland

Published by
Macdonald Publishers
Edgefield Road, Loanhead, Midlothian

ISBN 0 904265 16 1

*The publisher acknowledges the financial
assistance of the Scottish Arts Council
in the publication of this volume.*

Printed in Scotland by
Macdonald Printers (Edinburgh) Limited
Edgefield Road, Loanhead, Midlothian EH20 9SY

Foreword

THIS VOLUME was first proposed at the memorial service held for Douglas Young at St Andrews in January 1974. We should like to thank most heartily all the subscribers to the Memorial Volume Appeal Fund and to apologise for having kept them waiting so long. We can only hope that they will now feel pleasure in being reminded of their old friend's ways and words.

The selection of excerpts from the really vast amount of material which Douglas left behind him was no easy task: he himself said sometime before his death, and with truth, that he must have written millions of words. In the compilation of the memoir we are very grateful to those who have contributed reminiscences from which we have been given permission to quote: the Hon. Lord Robertson, Professor Hugh Seton-Watson, Miss N. V. Dunbar, Miss Deedra Mason, Professor W. J. Slater and Mr Nigel Tranter.

Finally we would express our warmest thanks to the Scottish Arts Council for their generous financial help without which publication would have been impossible, and to our publishers for their constant courtesy, help and co-operation at every stage in the production of the book.

CLARA YOUNG
DAVID MURISON

ACKNOWLEDGEMENTS

Thanks are due to the editors and publishers who readily granted permission for the reproduction of the various extracts, more fully recorded in the headings to the appropriate passages:

William MacLellan, Glasgow
Hollis and Carter, London
The Scotsman, Edinburgh
The Glasgow Herald, Glasgow
Cassel and Co., London
Greece and Rome, Oxford University Press, Oxford
University of Oklahoma Press, Norman, Okla., U.S.A.

Contents

Douglas Young: a Memoir

TO REDUCE Douglas Young to the compass of some thirty pages is no small task and those who read them and knew him may well feel that the real man has still eluded them, but after a moment's reflection may conclude that this is not surprising. For if ever there was a man defied description, flouted the conventional expectations of him, had an unbounded interest in and knowledge of an extraordinary range of topics, mixed uninhibitedly with all sorts and conditions of men, held strong and outspoken views on many public questions, and acted so completely *à sa tête*, it was Douglas. And yet though he was superficially unpredictable, deeper down he was a man of consistent principles and loyalties, who, having made up his mind that what he was doing was right, would stick to it and not count the cost; he was utterly loyal to his friends, completely dependable once he had given his word, kind, courteous and considerate always, and, conspicuous above all his other good qualities, generous in his judgments and apparently quite incapable of bearing a grudge against those who were manifestly stabbing him in the back.

The following pages are meant to give some impressions of a remarkable man rather than a detailed life story, much of which in any case he told in that racy and amusing volume he wrote in 1950, *Chasing an Ancient Greek*, which helps to fill out the picture of him and will explain at some length his views and attitudes and tastes and for brevity's sake will be referred to as his autobiography.

He was born on 5th June 1913 at Tayport in Fife. His father, Stephen Young, worked for twenty-six years in India as a jute salesman and mercantile clerk for a large Dundee firm. His mother had made a special trip home for his birth as Stephen insisted on all their children being natives of Tayport. (In all she made twenty-six separate crossings between Scotland and India). When only a few weeks old Douglas was taken to his parents' large house at Jagatdal near Calcutta. In later life he enjoyed relating how, aged only two, he had saved his brother from a dangerous snake by shouting out "Dekho! Dekho!" until a servant rushed up to kill the beast with a large stick. He used to say jocularly that his first language was Urdu, having picked up words from his Indian nurses—no doubt resulting in a bilingualism which was a natural beginning for the later

9

polyglot with his Latin, Greek, French, German, Italian, English, Scots, Gaelic and a smattering of the Slavonic tongues.

In 1921 he was sent to Merchiston Castle School in Edinburgh, in the old tower once inhabited by John Napier, who invented an early form of logarithms. Lord Robertson who was his contemporary at Merchiston describes Douglas's school career.

"At this stage at the age of 9, Douglas was thin, weedy and short-sighted. Because of this he was never any good at ball-games, and his physique made him useless at Rugby football. About this time he had a serious accident which involved a severe injury to his head. In the way of small boys his contemporaries believed implicitly that this accident had in some way changed his brain for the better. I suspect the truth to be that —like Sir Walter Scott and John Buchan—Douglas spent the long period of enforced idleness after a serious illness in nourishing his imagination, developing his faculty for thought and contemplation and discovering the delights of reading. Thereafter he soared above all his contemporaries." Lord Robertson names the teachers who influenced them most, James Garvin in French, and Richard Killick, who introduced them to the beauties and grandeurs of English literature. Life at Merchiston was pretty Spartan but Douglas throve on it. Though in a class with much older boys, he stood up to them and was never bullied, partly because his elder brother was there to keep the peace but also because of his own character. "His personality was likeable and curiously formidable—he had human sympathy and perception, a great sense of fun and wit, and he never talked down to anyone. He was prepared to tackle anything, even if unfit, and to do his bit. He kept himself to himself, let things revolve around him, and never complained. He was sardonic and his humour infectious. He made no enemies and lived and let live." Besides an intensive course in the Classics they studied in their last year Scottish history and literature of the 17th and 18th centuries, read Boswell's *Tour* and Burns and closely investigated the career of Montrose.

"At this stage of his life Douglas was thus saturated with the past and so far as I remember had little interest in the politics or economics of the contemporary world. The 18th century was his favourite era. He was a traditionalist, a conservative, a *laudator temporis acti*. Of Scottish National-ism as a modern political force he had nothing but scorn, even contempt." At a school debate on the subject of Scottish Home Rule he spoke and voted against it, as "the Honourable Member for Wormit."

In 1929 he was made a school prefect but after a few months he asked to be demoted. "He did not want to wield authority and have to perform duties that were often uncongenial, taking responsibility and making decisions that involved and affected other people. He preferred to step out of the limelight into the wings, where he could cultivate his own pursuits. . . . In his last winter at school he developed for the first time an interest in military affairs, being appointed Company Quartermaster Sergeant of the O.T.C. Oddly enough, Douglas was very proud of this appointment and took his duties very seriously."

In 1930 he had reached the sixth form and the time of decision about his future education—always a difficult moment for a lad of seventeen. Family circumstances will usually determine the issue pretty quickly for a poor boy. Douglas was more fortunate in being able to choose between three universities, Cambridge, Oxford and St Andrews. He had passed the Entrance Examinations for all three as well as taking enthusiastically to golf, and with the flippancy of youth, which in his more sedate years he never quite lost, he plumped for St Andrews in preference to Oxford or Cambridge, where there were no good golf courses. But another more serious reason seems to have influenced his choice, to which he alludes in his *Chasing an Ancient Greek*, "a sort of Nationalist instinct," that involved him in Eric Linklater's candidature on behalf of the Scottish National Party in a bye-election in East Fife in 1933 and brought him much notoriety later.

Anyhow he entered bejant at St Andrews and there can be no doubt that he never regretted it, that he formed an affection for his first Alma Mater that grew deeper with the years and survived some later experiences that might have embittered a less generous man. The Classics school at St Andrews has been distinguished by a series of outstanding scholars and in the thirties the professors were H. J. Rose in Greek and W. M. Lindsay in Latin. Rose was a complete extrovert who had read omnivorously, pontificated on any topic, relying on a prodigious memory which some-times let him down. But he taught with a zest and an abandon that carried his students along with him. Lindsay was almost the exact opposite, a reserved man cut off from his students by being stone deaf, but an old-fashioned scholar of the most exact and rigorous sort. Each in his own way imbued their young disciple with a larger enthusiasm for the Classics and a surer understanding of the methods of academic research. Besides getting all the main prizes, the Miller Prize for the most distinguished graduate of the year in Arts, the Guthrie Scholarship, and the Lewis Campbell Medal for Greek, he gave up golf for gardening and took to reading books on all kinds of subjects "to answer," as he said, "my own questions, not other people's." He was active in the Literary Society and, astonishing as it may seem, though not to Douglas, he became president of the Conservative Club. When rallied on this later, he used to say that politics had never been taken seriously in St Andrews since the Jacobite Rising of 1715.

It was at St Andrews that he won the nickname of "God," or, somewhat more reverently, "the Deity." The story goes that he was sitting reading a newspaper in the Common Room when he became aware of two fellow students beside him in an animated discussion on some political question of the time; they had reached an impasse in their speculations and one, stuck for an answer to some question posed by the other, which Douglas overheard, murmured, "God knows," whereupon Douglas laid down his paper and said with emphasis, "Well, *I* know, and I shall tell you," and proceeded to expound. Several letters beginning "Dear God" survive from his Oxford days. (Legend also has it that once while playing charades Douglas was carried into the room upside down: the clue was *dog*.)

But he left St Andrews with the pleasantest memories and a rich and well-stored mind eager for more. And he had incidentally savoured the delights of foreign travel by a visit to the Salzburg Festival (he played the piano and was especially fond of Mozart) and Budapest; and from then on the wanderlust never left him. So now he matures into the typical Scots student with wide general interests, knowing something about a great deal rather than a great deal about not very much.

With his first graduation behind him and a scholarship for further study, he gained an Open Exhibition at New College, Oxford, and entered on the usual philological, historical and philosophical disciplines which Oxford prescribes for its Classical students, Mods. and Greats. For all the prestige of Oxford and the undoubted eminence of its dons, of whom Douglas mentions with special regard and affection Professors Sir Maurice Bowra and A. H. Smith, and despite carrying off the First Craven Scholarship in 1935 and the Craven Research Fellowship in 1938, and honourable mentions for the Hertford Scholarship, the Chancellor's Latin Verse Prize, and for the Ferguson Scholarship for Classics for Scotland, he did not really like the place. The company was congenial, especially among his fellow Scots over whose Society he presided for a time, and he made many friends in his usual fashion, but the climate, humid in summer and damp in winter, made him actually ill after the bracing winds of St Andrews. "I went away after four years without regret, and have since gone back only to see people, not the place."

But Oxford did stimulate his interest in politics. He had been in Germany when Hitler came to power and had been made deeply aware of the importance of foreign affairs, and he became president of the Bryce Society whose special interest was in that very subject. It was there incidentally that he met the last Chancellor of the Weimar Republic, Brüning, who regaled him with stories about President Hindenburg's last years and how he received little support from Britain and France against the growing menace of Nazism. In 1935 his political sympathies veered leftwards, he joined the Labour Party and helped in canvassing for their candidate in a local bye-election, presumably on the strength of his experiences with the Nationalists earlier in Fife. But he did not abandon the earlier allegiance and as a voter in the old Scottish Universities constituency, he supported the S.N.P. and Professor Dewar Gibb against the victorious Ramsay MacDonald who had to be found a new seat after his old friends had contumeliously rejected him.

His fellow-collegian, Professor Hugh Seton-Watson, remembers the first time he met Douglas, "he held forth about Hungary, which he had then visited but I had not; but I knew something about it because of my father's long association with, and antagonism to, Hungarian nationalism. From that time on, over the years, we talked and argued about almost anything under the sun. His strange appearance, erudition and curiosity, directness and kindness attracted all sorts around him in Oxford, as elsewhere. He had an extraordinary charm which would quickly win over even those who at first reacted against his unconventional manner. It was difficult for anyone to be angry with him, even if they disagreed strongly; but the wide range of his interests did cause some to underrate him as a dilettante—in which, imprisoned by the pieties of Oxford specialism, by the time-honoured boundaries between branches of learning, they showed poor judgment and damaged themselves rather than him."

Lord Robertson who paid him a visit at Oxford in 1935 saw him from a somewhat different aspect. "I tracked him down in his rooms at the top of a high staircase in New College. I hardly recognised him. He had grown several inches in every direction; he was now a broad, strong giant of a man, with a black beard and a handsome head. I found him draped in tartan, wearing a broad-brimmed black hat, and blowing Hebridean airs on a recorder. He had undergone a physical and physiological change of late development, and was barely recognisable as the slight and subdued 17-year-old I had known so intimately at Merchiston. He was now an extrovert, and Oxford seemed to be turning him into an eccentric. I have always thought that his period at Oxford was an unrewarding and frustrating time for him."

His Oxford days drew to a close in 1938 and again a decision about his future faced him. Four alternatives came his way; he could have gone to the U.S.A. to a teaching or research post, as he was urged to do by the Warden of New College, the historian H. A. L. Fisher; he had a chance to go archaeologising with Leonard Woolley in Syria; he had the Craven Scholarship which could have kept him at Oxford or taken him on research where he wanted; and finally he was offered a job as assistant to the Professor of Greek at Aberdeen, the lowest of all academic posts in Scotland, on a three-year basis.

Self-interest might have suggested that the last was the least likely to lead to advancement and that a divorce from Oxford meant in effect the repudiation of the many benefices in all walks of life which Oxford has in its gift. But Douglas was not made that way as time was to prove. He had come to live with the Classics (the Craven Scholarship is awarded, in the terms of its founder, "for Classical learning and taste"), he wanted to pass on the knowledge and love of them as a teacher, and finally he had become increasingly aware of his essential Scottishness, as before in his choice of St Andrews. So in the autumn of 1938 he came to Aberdeen. Some of his friends used to tell him in banter that Aberdeen saved his soul, that if he had continued at Oxford he would have turned into a jelly of learned aestheticism, and he would demur to this sweeping statement with but half-hearted conviction for there was a grain of truth in it. He got comfortable digs in the medieval surroundings of Old Aberdeen near the Cathedral, which must have reminded him of St Andrews, and took to Aberdeen with real enthusiasm; and after a suitable interval the canny Aberdonians having weighed him up and found him far from wanting, took to him. The rumour that he taught Greek caused a confusion in the minds of the non-academic population who thought he was indeed a Greek, an error perhaps excusable when they saw him, the whole six feet six of him, splaying along the High Street with his long black beard and his big black velour hat to crown all. He used to tell a story of himself, similarly attired and walking along Oxford Street in London, hearing a man say to his companion in an unmistakable Glasgow accent, "Yon's a Cossack," and shouting back at him, "Cossack yersel!" to the man's utter astonishment.

As he became more familiar to the Aberdonians, they responded in an equally friendly and even jovial manner, and when he finally left the town, the natives felt that a virtue had gone out of them. He made an equal impression on his students who had never seen a teacher so much out of the usual ruck before and warmed quickly to his wit, learning and friendliness, appreciating above all the genuine interest he had in their welfare, an interest which became all the more marked and sympathetic when war broke out and they were swept one by one into the services, and was followed by deep grief when he heard that this or that one would never come back. His poem *Alasdair* quoted below is an elegy for one of these.

When he took to writing poetry seriously is not altogether clear. At ten or eleven he chronicled family occasions in McGonagall style. At seventeen during a summer holiday in Sutherland—he had with him dozens of poets from Aeschylus to Robert Bridges—his father asked him if he could write a poem, one which an editor would print. He replied, "Probably, what editor?" Lying at random in the hotel was a copy of *Chambers's Journal*. His father promised him a typewriter if he could get one printed in that magazine. Within a short time he was using it to type out Latin proses for W. M. Lindsay.

In the following few years he produced a very spasmodic output of verse and translations. But between the years 1935 and 1939 he had the good fortune to know Edwin and Willa Muir who were then living in St Andrews and Douglas went frequently to breakfast with them and submitted his verses to Muir, a judicious and penetrating critic, for whom Douglas had the highest regard and affection, no less warmly reciprocated. There is no doubt that he derived much pleasure and profit from this friendship which lasted as long as the Muirs lived. One of the questions much exercising him at this time was the use of Scots for poetry and the possibility of recreating it for prose and he and his like-minded colleague in the Greek Department at Aberdeen, David Murison, later the Editor of the Scottish National Dictionary, put out some numbers of a typewritten periodical, called by Douglas "The Auld Aiberdeen Courant and Neo-Caledonian Spasmodical," written mostly in Scots and sold in aid of a war charity, in which the subject and the name "Lallans," used by Burns and Stevenson, were revived for this new experimental Scots, of which Douglas became the protagonist in the years to come. In November 1940 he went to Perth and introduced himself to William Soutar, who had already produced much good verse in Scots, and Soutar records this in his diary as follows: "A Douglas Young introduced himself about 11 o'clock this morning—an exceedingly tall fellow with a shovel-beard—his leanness, longness and fringiness gave one the impression of a B.B.C. announcer who had partially metamorphosed into an aerial: a fluent talker with a lectorial style: didn't just get his wave-length." As he got to know him better Soutar enjoyed his visits (the last one just a few days before Soutar died), and in June 1943 he writes, "Douglas Young stalked in: monologue for the rest of the afternoon, which suited me—Douglas, though something of a conversational conveyor-belt, isn't a bore."

He often used to call Auld Aiberdeen his second spiritual home, and of course he came to it at a time of great ferment, when every mind was turned with anxiety to what Hitler's next move would be. The University Senior Common Room summed up events daily in what it took to be an informed manner, based chiefly on a reading of the *Times*, which was in those days singularly off the mark as the event showed, and Douglas pontificated with the best of them. Political meetings were frequent and were well attended by the worried and among them a small but active group of the S.N.P. to whom Douglas attached himself and was welcomed for his political expertise and his fluency as a public speaker. What all this led to is best told in his own words from his autobiography quoted below.

While he was in Aberdeen and the war was at one of its critical stages with the Germans overrunning Norway, the British Secret Service momentarily panicked and early one morning descended on several prominent Nationalists in various parts of Scotland to raid their homes for seditious or treasonable articles. Douglas was one of these and his voluminous correspondence—he kept every letter he received as well as a copy of every letter he sent—was carted off with himself to the Aberdeen police office. What the police made of Douglas's poetry, his notes on Greek textual criticism, his correspondence with foreigners about the sights, the art treasures, the history and antiquities of their native towns or the merits of their wines, their cuisine or their writers, is not recorded but it is to be hoped that they were edified as well as diverted. Douglas was released later in the day and his papers were soon returned intact. His more serious argument with the law was to come later. Sufficient to say that Aberdeen was a turning-point in his life and that he had the liveliest memories of his experiences there and of the many friends who remember him with equal vividness and pleasure.

When his three-year contract had expired, he was already in defiance of the authorities over conscription and had retired to Lochwinnoch in Renfrewshire to Meikle Cloak, the farm of the veteran Scottish Nationalist, R. E. Muirhead, who was very sympathetic to Douglas's attitude. It was here he met his wife-to-be, Helena Auchterlonie, and wrote much of his verse, contributed to various newspapers and periodicals, *Forward, The*

Scots Independent, etc., got on with his Greek studies, now concentrated on the 6th century poet Theognis, "the ancient Greek" of his autobiography, and waited for the authorities to act. But in the midst of his wrangle with the Ministry of Labour, the question of conscription in Scotland, not only of men for military service but also of women for industrial labour, chiefly in England, as well as the political tactics of the then Secretary of the S.N.P., John MacCormick, had caused a split in the Party. While he was waiting for the hearing of his appeal against his prison sentence, one of the factions put Douglas up for Chairman in opposition to the sitting member, the elderly journalist William Power. To the general surprise, Douglas's supporters carried the day and the MacCormickites left the Party to found the Scottish Convention. A few days later, however, the law took its course, his appeal was dismissed, Douglas was carried off to jail in Edinburgh, and the S.N.P. had to rebuild its fortunes without its Chairman, who was incidentally at the same time a member of the Labour Party.

Douglas bore this unpleasant experience with equanimity and made the best of his incarceration by keeping up with his studies and by writing as he was permitted to do. On St Andrew's Day 1942 he made a Scots version of the twenty-third metrical psalm, and as far as was possible in the circumstances supervised the publication of his first volume of poems *Auntran Blads* to which Hugh MacDiarmid wrote a strongly commendatory foreword.

There followed his release, his marriage, his candidature in a Parliamentary bye-election in Kirkcaldy where he came a good second with over forty per cent of the poll. Obviously the people of Kirkcaldy did not think his attitude as absurd and disloyal as the powers that were did. When he was again conscripted, this time for industrial work, and again refused, the whole process began all over again and Douglas found himself in prison for the second time. Sir Compton MacKenzie later described this episode in some detail in his book, *On Moral Courage*. Now it became obvious that the politicians were being merely vindictive and the fact gained him much more sympathy than condemnation. The stand he took, however unpopular it seemed, was by no means futile; it served to bring home to the Scots some deep and unresolved issues in their situation, and now, more than thirty-five years after, the Scottish Nationalists, with their case half conceded, must recognise that Douglas struck a brave blow for their cause.

He was far too generous a spirit to bear a grudge against anyone for all this. He faced the consequences of his action with open eyes and took it all cheerfully enough but there is no doubt that some iron entered his soul, and that he began to learn who were real friends and who were not, a lesson that was to be repeated in later years.

With the end of the war and a family of two daughters on his hands he made his way to Edinburgh to see what would turn up and to enjoy its metropolitan atmosphere, its libraries, art galleries, theatres, and so forth. Early in 1946 the Chair of Greek at Glasgow fell vacant with the retirement of Professor William Rennie and Douglas put his name forward, with testimonials from dons at St Andrews and Oxford, and from Edwin Muir and James Bridie (Dr O. H. Mavor) and a certificate from the former Secretary of State for Scotland, Tom Johnston, that he had continued his classical studies with diligence during his incarceration—a rather unorthodox medley of referees. This was certainly chancing his long arm to its fullest extent and he took the further step of answering anticipated criticisms:

> In my view of the possibility that my political activities may be misunderstood or regarded as a disqualification for academic work, I should like to recall that the ancient Greeks were notoriously a politically-minded people, and went so far as to term 'idiots' all those among them who took no part in public affairs. Accordingly, some experience of political life may be thought useful to an exponent of Greek culture.
>
> Further, as the ancient Greeks were especially zealous for Constitutionalism in politics, it may be worth mentioning that my own participation in public life has arisen mainly through my interest in democratic Constitutionalism. I have edited with a commentary the Treaty of Union governing the relations of Scotland and England, and have personally fought in the High Court of Justiciary cases founded upon that constitutional instrument—well-founded in the view of legal persons acquainted with the matter.
>
> Moreover, my constitutional principles have received widespread public support, reflected partly in Parliamentary elections. In this connection the Regius Professor of Greek in the University of Aberdeen is willing to testify that while I served as his assistant I never extended my political activities to the class-room.
>
> In view of the decline in the study of Greek in Scotland it may be thought well to appoint in a Scottish University personalities who are

able not only to cultivate exact scholarship but also to act as popular exponents among the general.

There was nothing conciliatory about this or, in the climate of the times, very diplomatic. He was sticking to his guns and in fact firing off a few salvos at the Establishment as it then was. What the Appointments Committee said to this is not recorded. The Chair was given to A. W. Gomme, a senior member of the Glasgow Department with a distinguished record as a Greek historian. A second attempt to join Gomme's staff also failed, but apparently as a kind of consolation prize a lectureship in Scottish literature was later offered to him, but it coincided with his appointment to Dundee and he chose the job in Classics.

It might be interesting at this point to quote some of the things his referees had to say about him, as they are in the main both apt and shrewd and in fact were substantiated by his subsequent career. Professor Rose wrote: "Mr Young is without exception or doubt the most brilliant student I have ever taught. No one else has shown so much originality, backed with as much self-won knowledge. He always gives the impression of knowing far more than is necessary for his immediate purpose and his application of what he knows is always his own. He is also completely free of narrow pedantry, keenly alive to the happenings of the world around him, and, perhaps most important of all to a historian, possessed of strong opinions on all sorts of matters. He will never shut himself up within the limits of one part of his subject or remain indifferent to or be ignorant of the broader fields of learning beyond." The Warden of his Oxford college calls him "for his age, learned to an exceptional degree. His Classical record at Oxford has been distinguished, and would have been still more distinguished but for the width and diffusion of his intellectual interests. Mr Young would certainly impress his pupils as being a sound scholar, and a very clever and ingenious man, with a nice turn of wit and plenty of fancy. He is much liked by all who know him." His tutor, Mr E. C. Yorke, writes in similar terms: "I have never had a pupil whom it has been a greater pleasure and profit to teach. He is learned, but no pedant, and takes a lively interest in people and things about him."

His first interest had been in Greek history rather than literature. The allusions to his diffusion of interests are explained by such things as his reading through the whole of the works of Polybius, a historian who does not usually bulk largely in college examinations and who is often little more than a mere name even to many Hellenists but in whose discursive treatment of history Douglas seemed to find a particular pleasure. Indeed, in such works as his story of St Andrews and Edinburgh he is not unlike Polybius himself, with perhaps a dash of Herodotus and Pausanias. He started off on his research on a history of Boeotia and it was only later that he switched to Theognis.

After two years he found the sort of job he wanted in Scotland in the academic world as assistant lecturer in Latin at University College, Dundee, then part of his old university of St Andrews. The head of the Department, W. L. Lorimer, who thought highly of Douglas's scholarship, had much sympathy also with his nationalist views and wanted to appoint him, had some difficulty in overcoming opposition to his candidate but the committee also were for him, and so he came to Dundee and in a short time transferred his home to his native town of Tayport. He enjoyed Dundee, though some of the Latin presented for his criticism made him wince not infrequently (two of his female students regularly got minus fifty for their proses: after extensive coaching he was happy to be able to raise their marks to zero!), but he had a great deal of fun too, shared with his students. Another young lady found it necessary to take her dog into the classroom every day, where the animal co-operated with the work of the class in so seemly and douce a manner that Douglas presented him at the end of the session with a certificate of merit in dog-Latin.

This same year, 1947, Douglas found a new interest. He had become a member of P.E.N. by virtue of his poetry (he had published his second volume that year, *A Braird o Thristles*) and as a representative of Scotland he attended the conference in Zürich, and made the acquaintance of many of the world's leading writers. Next year it was in Copenhagen and the year after that in Venice, where there were incidentally some manuscripts of Theognis to inspect. The Venetian meeting is described in great detail in his autobiography with not a few salty remarks on the behaviour of various delegates and some brilliant description of the sights of Venice and the Lombard countryside. He liked talking to all and sundry and was always a responsive and patient listener but even he could become bored with the appalling egotism of some cliques of writers who swarm to those literary jamborees, and had to seek refuge from time to time in a medieval church or a restaurant. P.E.N. Congresses became almost an annual event and he visited Russia in 1952, where he met among others Marshak, the writer of children's stories and the translator of Burns, and Bulgakov, Tolstoy's last secretary.

In 1957 he was made the Scottish P.E.N. President, a post which he held for four years. It is of interest to include at this point a brief appreciation of Douglas by Nigel Tranter. He writes:

It was my privilege, and also my problem, to succeed Douglas Young as President of the Scottish Centre of International P.E.N. It was always a problem for anyone to succeed Douglas in anything. It was not difficult to *follow* him, as a leader—for he was a born leader; but to succeed him in that leadership was something very different. I fear that the members of P.E.N. felt the sudden change of temperature quiet acutely.

This sense of inadequacy was particularly noticeable on international occasions—and one of the P.E.N. Club's principal functions is the closer association of writers of all countries. Everyone automatically looked up when Douglas entered the room, however large or crowded. And not only on account of his height and dramatic appearance; nor even only because of his reputation as poet, scholar, author, linguist, raconteur and fighter of causes. His was a personality which sparkled, even flashed—for although the most genial of men, he could be roused, authoritative, angry, even devastating, on occasion. Since he remained an active member of P.E.N. and continued to attend its functions after his retirement from the presidency—as all would have been greatly disappointed had he not—I fear that many, especially foreigners, looked upon him as Scotland's representative and spokesman for long after a lesser figure, with few of these qualities, had replaced him. Which, of course, was all to the good of Scotland and for P.E.N., and often a major relief for his successor. To many a foreign writer, I think, Douglas *was* Scottish P.E.N.

My memories of him cover a long period, for I knew him long before the P.E.N. days, both of us being actively involved in the early struggles towards self-government for Scotland, immediately after the Second World War. Always he was a man to be reckoned with, a man to be liked, admired and appreciated—even if one disagreed with him. He was the last man to let that affect good relations. For one with such definite and vehement views on all subjects, it was amazing how popular he remained, how everybody enjoyed his company. A man more *alive* would be hard to imagine, a knowledgeable enthusiast in an age when such are rare indeed.

It is tragic that in his last years Scotland found so little use for his many talents that he had to spend so much of his time outwith this country. It was very much to Scotland's loss.

21

Edwin Muir recalled that he received a visit from Douglas in Rome during the 1961 P.E.N. conference. They discussed the fortunes of Lallans about which Muir was never enthusiastic. "From Douglas," he wrote, "I got the impression that the Lallans poets weren't doing as well as they expected. I have no ill-will towards them, but they never seemed to me to be very gifted, except for Grieve." Douglas however persevered with his Lallans. Other Scottish writers, notably Robert Kemp, had been successful with Scots versions of foreign plays and poems, and Douglas had already produced a deservedly praised rendering of Valéry's *Cimetière Marin*. Now he turned his hand to the comedies of Aristophanes and in 1958 wrote *The Puddocks* for the students of St Andrews to put on in the Byre Theatre. It was very well received and its promoters were emboldened to try it out on the Fringe of the Edinburgh Festival that same year. It was staged in the Braidburn Open Air Theatre where the burn itself flows down in front of the proscenium to represent the Styx and the chorus of frogs could perform their antics in the water in a most realistic manner. Unfortunately weather conditions made things unpleasant for players and audience alike, the acoustics were bad, and the play did not quite come off, despite the felicities of the translation. It was found incidentally that the language was little of a barrier for non-Scots who, helped by the action, soon picked their way through what was being said. In 1959 Douglas tried again with a Scots version of the *Birds* for the Fringe but this was extremely amateurishly produced and completely flopped. But in 1966 it was revived and given the full honours of the official Festival at the Lyceum Theatre. Again the translation was good, though perhaps not so consistently so as in *The Puddocks*, and the production had some excellencies, especially in the costumes and setting, but the critics gave it a mixed reception. The audiences, however, generally enjoyed it and the scholars found the production "amazingly faithful to the spirit of the original Greek."

In 1953 with the rationalisation of the various departments and faculties between St Andrews and its Dundee College, the Latin department was closed down, W. L. Lorimer was appointed to the Greek Chair in succession to Rose, and Douglas, having been given the choice, opted to transfer to Greek instead of continuing in Latin, as he was now immersed in his study of Theognis and had the chance of picking up the threads again from Aberdeen. This he found particularly congenial, and these years seem to have been among the happiest of his career, teaching in his old university, living at home with his family in his native town, and participating to the full in the political and cultural life of his own country.

He had remained Chairman of the Scottish National Party till 1945 but began to have some misgivings about the Party's chances of early success. He had always taken the view that the S.N.P. should be as far as possible an all-party coalition, presumably a coalition against the Conservative Party, which was uncompromisingly unionist, and this, in practice, if not in theory, had been the MacCormick line. This argument was strongly supported by his old friend, R. E. Muirhead, former Secretary of the Scottish Home Rule Association, which had formed a common platform for Liberal, Labour and I.L.P. leaders, Trade Unions and Co-operatives and many local authorities, but had never acted as a political party putting up candidates against any other party but sponsored the bill framed by the Rev. James Barr to be put through Parliament by the Labour Party in opposition after 1926. Challenge at the polls however was the policy of the National Party of Scotland, started by MacCormick and others in 1928, and joined by Muirhead to his own later frequently expressed regret. This new party started to fight elections and thus antagonised those members of the Liberal and Labour Parties who had a general sympathy with their aims. But the S.N.P. made little headway itself for many years and MacCormick in fact was proposing a reversion to the old Home Rule Association stance in 1942 when his leadership was challenged and defeated by Dr Robert McIntyre and his following and by the election of Douglas as Chairman. McIntyre felt his policy was justified by his own election as the first Scottish Nationalist M.P. for Motherwell in 1945 during the electoral wartime truce between the main British parties. This encouraged many of the old N.P.S. members who had left the later S.N.P. or been expelled under the MacCormick regime and the more intransigent nationalists began to return in force till in 1948 they succeeded in getting the S.N.P. to change its constitution to exclude from its own membership members of any other party, thus precluding the Common Front approach, on the general grounds that divided allegiances had got and would continue to get the Scottish cause nowhere.

Douglas, who had pinned his colours to a resuscitation of "Barr's Bill" to be again promoted by the Labour Party in office, disagreed strongly with this new move and was *ipso facto* disqualified from remaining in the S.N.P. So it was back to the Labour Party for him and a constant canvassing, with no success, with his new associates for Barr's Bill. He clung tenaciously to the fact that Scottish Labour conferences had genuflected from time to time to the old slogan of Home Rule for Scotland, which they had inherited *inter alia* from Keir Hardie, and that various leaders, including Attlee, had made non-committal noises to the same general purport. All this is expounded in Douglas's book *Scotland*, written in 1971 after the marked advance of the S.N.P.'s fortunes, and it will be noted that he is as heavily critical of the Labour Party for its performance in the British, as well as the Scottish, spheres, as he is of the other parties, and that he is much less convinced of his party's sincerity over Home Rule. He has not lived to see that his pessimism about the progress of the S.N.P. was unfounded; on the other hand, he would have approved, no doubt with much wry amusement, of the Labour Party's new-found enthusiasm for something much less than halfway to Barr's Bill.

Life went on in a fairly even tenor at St Andrews, though of course at a tempo which would prostrate the ordinary man, taking his students through the textual complications of a Greek play, coaching them in the writing of Greek prose, rushing off to this or that place to take part in a B.B.C. discussion or chair a meeting of P.E.N. or some other body, or to speak on some political platform, usually by invitation of a local Labour Party, delivering harangues on Lallans and literature to cultural groups such as the Saltire Society of which he was an active member, proposing Immortal Memories at Burns Suppers, contributing articles to all sorts of periodicals on all sorts of subjects of which examples are given below, writing a thrice weekly column on Scottish topics to the London daily, the *News Chronicle*. The energy, mental and physical, needed for all this is quite astounding, but he kept himself physically fit, especially by swimming of which he was very fond, by rising at a very early hour and getting in a good deal of work before most of the lieges were astir and while his mind was at its most alert. The preliminary check-list of his writings printed in this volume gives a good idea of the amount of his outpourings and their variety between the years 1940 and 1973, and this of necessity does not include ephemeral newspaper articles and letters of which there was no dearth either. The most important of his surviving papers now occupy 48 linear feet on the shelves of the National Library of Scotland.

In 1955 W. L. Lorimer retired from the Chair of Greek and Douglas applied for the vacancy but was turned down by his Alma Mater in favour of K. J. Dover, a Fellow of Balliol, who after twenty-one years has returned to be the President of Corpus Christi College, Oxford.

Douglas continued in the Department and became Senior Lecturer in 1960. Summer vacations were mostly spent chasing the Ancient Greek in his manuscripts in various libraries and monasteries in Paris, Rome,

Milan, Venice, Florence, Munich, Vienna and London. He had decided to submit his studies in Theognis to the University as a thesis for the degree of D.Litt., in conjunction with the edition of the poet which he had been invited to prepare for the famous German series of Classical texts by Teubner of Leipzig. This appeared, dedicated to W. M. Lindsay, in 1961 and was well received by the pundits who however remarked on the extreme conservatism of his text and his manifest reluctance to depart from the manuscripts, a trait that Douglas was to show later on in his treatment of Aeschylus, whose plays have a notoriously difficult tradition. Towards the end of 1962 the thesis was upheld and he graduated Dr Young next January. In September 1963 he crossed the Atlantic for the first time and found America intensely stimulating. He had been invited for a sabbatical year to lecture as a visiting professor at the University of Minnesota, where he began to sample the better endowed life on an American campus. Probably about this time the thought must have occurred to him that perhaps it might be possible to reconcile the wish to remain in Scotland with the greater facilities for study and travel in America and, it must be freely admitted, the greater encouragement for academic distinction and the more rewarding response from students who are really dedicated and interested in what one has to teach them. After all the trans-Atlantic session is somewhat shorter and there would be about half the year to spend in Scotland or Europe. After his strong candidature for the vacant Greek chair at Aberdeen had been unsuccessful in 1965, he felt free to consider some job offers which were arriving from universities in the new world. His lecture tours while based at Minneapolis had caused some stir. In 1968 the chance came of a Classics chair at McMaster University, Hamilton, Ontario. But his last act of pietas to his Alma Mater was one of his best books, *St Andrews, Town and Gown, Royal and Ancient*, published in March 1968.

A subsidiary attraction was the opportunity to study the constitutional system of Canada with the division of powers between the Federal and the Provincial parliaments and the more fissiparous tendencies of Quebec, which have obvious analogies with the situation of Scotland and Great Britain, and what might have seemed pure academic theory in 1969 has become a very real and pragmatic problem in 1977. In a newspaper interview in this same year he said that a separate Scottish Parliament was inevitable in the logic of history: "It doesn't matter how far you go in the end; the first stage is a Scottish Parliament with powers that include the present Secretary of State's. He already represents four departments rolled into one, Home Secretary, Education, Agriculture and Health. A separate Scottish Government would be financed by annual votes of supply in the Commons. Then the Ministry of Works could be transferred one year, Fuel and Power another. As I see it, it would be a gradual process without interfering with any advantages we enjoy under the present set-up." Possibly an unbiased study of these suggestions might have saved some of the worst gaffes of recent political démarches on the subject.

After a pleasant holiday in Italy and Spain he left for Canada as an émigré Scot in September 1968. The session was punctuated with visits to California, Texas, and Chapel Hill, North Carolina, where a new chair of Greek had been just endowed by a cultured plutocrat called Paddison. Tentative offers of it were made to him by the University and he apparently pondered the matter for some time, no doubt having some misgivings about leaving Hamilton so soon. He was still undecided in December 1969 but by Easter he was again at Chapel Hill as professor-elect to look for accommodation, having resigned his Canadian chair and canvassed successfully for his successor to be his old St Andrews student, W. J. Slater.

When some of his old friends expressed their regrets that he was leaving Scotland, he had pointed out that he was still firmly anchored in Tayport and that he would in fact be able to see Scotland better from a more detached vantage point. In any case he was already planning a book on Scotland which was to run to over 250 pages and which with his apparently inexhaustible energy he contrived to write in his cis-Atlantic intervals in 1969-70. It appeared in the summer of 1970 and is, like most of Douglas's books, densely packed with information, data and statistics; it is a vade-mecum to the state of contemporary Scotland. That it was less successful than his books on Edinburgh and St Andrews became clear fairly soon to Douglas himself who thought its issue was rather mistimed by the publishers, but the real trouble seems to have been that events in Scotland had now reached a momentum of change that even he could not keep pace with and much of it was out of date before it appeared. Nevertheless, there is a great deal in it invaluable for reference and written with his usual wit and raciness.

Having now finished Theognis, he turned his attention to Aeschylus on whom he had been lecturing for many years and this led to more manuscript hunting in Italy, Spain and Greece. In 1971 he was at Mount Athos on such an expedition which his companion, Professor Slater, thus describes:

We were busy by then trying to catch Father Athanasius, who among many other offices also held that of librarian, obviously with no enjoyment. He made it clear that visitors, especially those looking for pagan manuscripts, were not welcome to him even though the tall bearded one carrying the black umbrella might indeed look like a patriarch. Grudgingly the library was opened for us, a low stone building with heavily barred windows in a corner of the courtyard. At last Triclinius' manuscript of Aeschylus. Douglas seized it and carried it off to the light muttering 'Interesting, very interesting.' That was all he was ever to see of it, for Father Athanasius took the book quickly back and locked it in its case. No amount of protestations, entreaties, offers to read under supervision availed. No, there was not enough personnel to watch a foreigner read a page of manuscript. We had come a long way? Too bad, there were too many visitors anyway. Douglas, almost apoplectic with rage, had to be placated and Father Athanasius thought that this was best achieved by showing him the robe once worn—or so he said—by the monastery's founder; and since this only produced even greater signs of apoplexy, the final treasure was revealed —a medallion which gave its wearer the power to walk on water. No words can describe the patriarchal wrath at being offered these treasures. Achilles did not reject Agamemnon's offer with greater contempt. I hastily manoeuvred the infuriated bard outside as he was attempting all too clearly to make known his new-found equation of barbarism with Byzantine monkhood.

He was very pensive at dinner that evening in the hotel at Ouranopolis and recited for me 'Sailing to Byzantium' very movingly. He hated growing old, and the line 'An aged man is but a paltry thing' he declaimed with such feeling that I was glad there was no one on the beach to hear us. Emotion, oddly enough for such a cultivated man, came readily to him, but also the verse and voice to express it. There were two highlights on that trip, one of which I have recounted—the mood of our evening after returning from Athos, when he expressed the antithesis between his Hellenism and its love of life and the gloomy rituals of a decayed Christianity that we had so recently left. The other came later when we climbed—illegally—up to the theatre in Delphi to see sunrise on the Pleistos valley before traffic and tourists disturbed the peace of the sacred place. He stood in the middle of the orchestra and declaimed Pindar's first Isthmian ode.

I have always felt that the greatest attributes of my late mentor were the unbounded enthusiasm for the ancient world and, what is rarer, his complete familiarity with its poetry. It came readily to his phenomenal memory. It illustrated his moods and graced his baroque locutions. Yet he wore it lightly, in an old-fashioned way, assuming in his unfortunate hearers the same familiarity as he possessed; and he inspired others to acquire it by his own example. Like many others of Douglas's students whom he took to Greece, I learned more about Hellenism from him than from the ruins or inscriptions that he showed us. Whether manuscripts on Athos or Pythian victories were the interest of the day, they came alive for us through the words of the ancients and through his vitality. He did not like the period of Greece's old age; and he would not himself have liked to see his own powers decline.'

His lectures on Aeschylus had a bye-product in a translation of the Oresteia published after his death though he had written the foreword in May 1973. In the introduction he comes down strongly for keeping to the texts as we have them handed down: "Far more harm has been done by unnecessary conjecture than by leaving alone and trying to interpret the manuscripts." The interesting thing about his version however is the "sprung rhythm" of his lines corresponding to the ordinary iambic trimeter of the Aeschylean dialogue—one might call it in Greek fashion logaoedic, and a more complex metrical system in the choral odes, which in an unusual and unconventional way gives an effective impression of what the Greek must have sounded to an Athenian audience, besides allowing for a literalness not usually achieved without sacrifice of style in English translations.

His friend and colleague at St Andrews, Miss Nan V. Dunbar, of Somerville College, Oxford, writes of his academic work: "He was an old-fashioned scholar in that he preferred to deal with technical questions of technical criticism and detailed exegesis rather than to indulge in what another old-fashioned scholar once called 'the gush aspect' of literary criticism. Some of his most valuable published work was the result of his patient investigation of the habits of scribes in the manuscript tradition of Aeschylus and of Pindar. His collations of two manuscripts of Aeschylus were used by Sir Denys Page for the new Oxford Classical Text of 1972." But his extreme conservatism of text

> ignored the demonstrable fact that scribes are often guilty of serious corruptions in which far more than a single letter is involved. There was sometimes a streak of rather perverse ingenuity which appeared to

overlook wider considerations of taste or even of common sense and which makes, most seriously, his Teubner text of Theognis less useful than it ought to have been. But by no means all his Greek scholarly work was narrowly technical. Perhaps his most memorable pieces, and probably the most enjoyable, are those on Homer. Here his knowledge of Gaelic poetic traditions enabled him to draw a telling analogy in favour of the 'premeditation' theory of Homeric composition as against the 'improvisation' theory, in the article 'Never blotted a line' in *Arion*, 1967, which in this respect has won praise even from scholars to whom the rest of the article was unpalatable.

As a teacher Douglas could be greatly stimulating for his abler students, who appreciated his gifts of vivid description, though sometimes even they could become restive under his unremitting attention to minute detail and (the old classical tradition again) his omission to give an overall view of the work on which he was lecturing; but his deep knowledge of the texts and his energetic gusto often proved highly infectious and would inspire students to go and find out a lot more about the work in question than they might have done after lectures giving a more finished and well-rounded account. He made a great impact on the American students of his last years, who were fascinated by his lecturing style with its combination of austere scholarship and irrepressible humour. He was extremely generous with time and trouble for any students who wished to go properly into a question, and would lend his detailed notes to help them. His voluminous reading threw up an unfailing stream of lively ideas and led him to have always several irons in the fire and at times to publish too quickly work which would have benefitted from longer reflection, so that many of his articles are a mixture of good and bad. He was always very generous over finding time to read and comment, often most helpfully and constructively, on work which colleagues asked him to look at.

The impression he created on his American students is fully described by one of them at Chapel Hill, Miss Deedra Mason:

He seemed on the surface at war with himself; there was warmth and reserve, approachability and distance—the latter, I think, involuntary but palpable. He was eccentric, ingenuous, enthusiastic, intense, as imposing physically as intellectually. An undeniable physical presence which dominated necessarily and naturally. We called him the Far Thunderer. He had such vitality that, until it happened, he and the very

29

notion of death were incompatible. What most distinguished him in class were two things: the first was a really wicked sense of humour whose source was less rancor than a justified pride ('When I was 17 I taught Rose Greek metrics.' 'Rose believed that in his own pronunciation he reproduced Greek accents, but all that went up and down were his eyebrows.' 'Though he knows better, our good editor includes this preposterous reading in the apparatus only because the man who suggested it was his teacher.' 'The French, they are inaccurate.' 'Now, Mr H. will read Greek as it is pronounced in Mississippi.' 'And now I will show you what Aeschylus himself wrote.' '*Corr.* in the apparatus here stands not for *correxit* but for *corrupit*') and with it came a delighted laugh and sparkling eyes. Part of his humour was his diction —or so it seemed to me—always of Graeco-Latin derivation, always exactly what he wanted to say. Who else would speak of dolicho-cephalous children or of one marching idiorhythmically for out of step? . . . The second thing that distinguished him in class was not a mere difference from other teachers, but *the* difference. He was the same man in his office, in the classroom, at his home, speaking to the APA; his manner never changed. It was this unity of man and work (and that was the secret to his charm and inaccessibility; the sheer joy of watching someone who was so very good at what he did doing what he loved best) that, I think, gave him some harmony and serenity and kept him intact despite his excessive energy—it let him combine phenomenally intense concentration with objectivity and wit. He could give us so much because there was such an overflow and because it represented no threat to his abundance and no challenge to him personally. . . . But so many apparent contradictions: I think he was something of a mystic. I would not be surprised to learn that he believed in telepathy [he did] and reincarnation—all that and a logical mind that never rested. I have sometimes wondered whether an intimation of an indecently early death may have been responsible for some of the vitality and energy.

And there is another simpler touching testimonial, sent to the department chairman while Douglas was still alive, from a non-Classics student:

Although a graduate student in economics, I enrolled in Professor Douglas Young's Greek I-II this past semester to learn not only about Attic Greek, but also about the cultural origins of Western civilisation and the values of humanistic study. I am happy to say that Dr Young, surely one of the finest teachers I have ever met, has been extremely effective in assisting me toward the realisation of both these goals. As a result of his influence I now *can* read Thucydides and, what is perhaps even more important, I now *want* to read Thucydides, and so I do—every night before falling off to sleep. A gracious patient man with a most delightful sense of humour, Dr Young has shown me how very much we economists lose when we cut ourselves off from the great literary-philosophical traditions of the past.

His last Greek assignment was the preparation of an edition of the first four books of the Odyssey for an Italian series. He had been working off and on at Homer for many years and had written various controversial articles (for which the bibliography below may be consulted) in favour of the unitarian theory as against the predominant modern tendency to assign the Iliad and the Odyssey to separate poets and to explain the construction of each poem in terms of oral improvisation. Another important commitment was his chairmanship of the advisory committee set up by the American Philological Association to help to organise the Thesaurus project—a multi-million dollar scheme aiming to produce a complete word list of the whole of the Ancient Greek language, to be retrievable by means of computers. The invitation to participate in this project was a due and just recognition of his academic eminence and it gave him a great amount of pleasure. He was looking forward to getting down to work during the session 1973-74 and set off for the U.S.A. in good health and spirits in September. On 23rd October he wrote home about arrangements for his wife to fly out in mid-November—his last letter. Next morning his neighbour heard him moving about his flat at his usual early hour but he failed to turn up for a seminar and a subsequent lecture, a telephone call was not answered and a messenger, despatched to find out what was wrong, found him dead at his desk, with his Homer in front of him.

A memorial service for him was held at Chapel Hill and later, on 12th January 1974, at St Andrews University.

Such in its outline was the life of Douglas Young. To sum him up is well-nigh impossible. He was a big man in every sense, physically, mentally and spiritually. He was conspicuous everywhere he went. People who came to him out of idle curiosity or amusement remained to listen and learn, captivated by his wit and erudition. He was a polymath, of course, with a fantastically well-stored mind, enriched by the widest reading, constant travel, and contacts with people of all lands and of all conditions, and he was always eager to learn more, which made him equally popular as a good listener. He lived according to Terence's maxim, that he was a man and there was nothing human which did not interest him. Sometimes he reminded one of a helicopter, for both literally and figuratively he would drop out of the skies from afar perpendicularly upon one, leave behind or carry off something, object or idea alike, and be airborne again before one quite realised what was happening. Possibly the Socratic gadfly would be a not inappropriate parallel.

Soaked as he was in Hellenism, his steps turned naturally and without conscious effort towards ἀρετή, which the Greek dictionaries tell us means excellence, more of active excellence than the strictly moral virtues, excellence in art, skill, and closely combined with this the notion of distinction. But not in the study only. His political career and writings are ample testimony to his dedication to the well-being in all things of his fellow-men, though unlike so many politicians, he got nothing out of it for himself and indeed his sympathies undoubtedly prejudiced his own personal advancement. But he took the larger view.

Professor Seton-Watson well says of him in this aspect:

At Oxford we both belonged to a dining club which was addressed from time to time by speakers on international affairs. After the meal a loving-cup was passed, and every member drank in turn to the toast *Der Weltbürger*. It seemed to me then a slightly portentous procedure; but if ever I have known a real *Weltbürger*, it was Douglas. His passionate devotion to the Scottish cause never for a moment clashed with his quality of true citizen of the world, not only of the republic of letters but also of a wider community.

In this, and in his extraordinary appetite for knowledge, appreciation of scholarship, and intellectual curiosity, he embodied, I think, a great Scottish tradition—not the tradition of provincial rancour, which plagues the Scots no less than it plagues other nations, but the tradition of the Edinburgh of Adam Smith and David Hume, which he so much admired, and in which, if he had lived two centuries earlier, he would have been at home. Scotland needs such men today. Europe too has few, and sorely needs them. Douglas was a good European as well as a good Scot; and he knew well many of the cities, landscapes, languages and peoples of Europe. Many who believe that they know and belong to European culture—and even some who really do know and belong—think that they can show how cultured they are by sneering at America and Americans. One of the things that most delighted me about Douglas in his later years (it did not surprise me, for I should have expected it of him) was his absolute rejection of such attitudes. Discovery of America (from Ontario and Minnesota to California and North Carolina) was for him a joyful and exciting enterprise, with plenty to arouse both amusement and admiration, and to stretch that insatiable curiosity of his. There he made many friends, and found intellectual equals and congenial spirits, with whom he could share his intellectual explorations, and a human warmth with which St Andrews was not always generous. There too there must be people whom, like myself, his going has left inconsolable.

Well, here is what another of his American students had to say about this:

His human insight in poetry, together with his broad technical knowledge of it, was important to me; he was endlessly interested in the diversity of language and of cultural features. I think his feeling for Scots nationalism became bound up with his concern for the cultural character of all people. As language may be thought of as a function or a representation of cultural and intrinsic traits, poetry was important as him a humanist. It is an invigorating memory to me that he had lately become interested in American history and in a sort of early American ethnography. But his insight went beyond broad ethnography to personalities and personal matters. He encouraged me to come to a better understanding of my family as a way to a clearer sense of myself. I have strong memories of him.

But amid his multiplicity of interests which came and went, there was one which never changed, his deep and abiding loyalty to his own native land. He knew it well from north to south and from east to west; he had studied Scotland's history and literature and language, not only as a professional scholar but as an amateur, in the original etymological sense of the word; he was proud to be of a long line of Scottish ancestors and to have been in his generation the heir of their best traditions; he saw in his own lifetime how these were threatened by the deadly forces of mass civilisation; he had a large share of the *praefervidum ingenium Scotorum* in him and in his own way he resisted those forces to his no small cost where he thought they were deployed against the freedom and identity of Scotland. If in return Scotland did so little for him, that is our loss more than his, and because his feelings for Scotland were so deep, he almost never showed what he felt about it. He went on serving the best interests of his country in the way in which circumstances permitted him. He stood up for principles and policies which however novel and unpopular at the time, have now become acceptable and likely to prevail, although he has not lived to see it. But readers may judge for themselves how prophetic his words were, and so we have used this memorial volume to recall them and the man who wrote them to his friends and to make sure that when the roll-call comes to be made of those who served Scotland well, his name may find a place of honour among them.

A Day and a Night in the Dolomites

Written in October 1933. An early prose essay, never published,
recalling one of the high-lights of a far-ranging European journey
during one of the Long Vacations.

AFTER A NIGHT in the hut on top of the Fedaia Pass, I strode down the Pian di Lobbia over a sward of sulphur anemone and the stemless gentian that squats upon its cushion and bluely trumpets to all the winds, and in the quaint inn nestling under the Pizzo Buda imbibed "Sciroppo di Lampone," a delicious concoction from the sweet little Alpine raspberries plucked by the sweet little Alpine cow-girls. Thus refreshed I started again and walked through a wondrous winding canyon of dripping limestone, rent apart to admit a noisy torrent that dashed from side to side, and a winding road crossing thereover by innumerable rustick bridges. For nearly a mile my course lay between these dank and rugged walls, made gracious with exquisite ferns and mosses and tufts of primulas and campanulas winking from every cleft and ledge; and high above sheep-like clouds strayed along the ragged blue ribbon of sky. From glistening grottos in the dark cliffs the Holy Mother of God beamed benignly amid wreaths of Edelweiss and Alpenrose culled by the devoted hands of the pious villagers.

On emerging from this gloomy sanctity, I cast off my clothes in quite an abandoned manner and sprawled joyously in the hot sun on an unshorn meadow. But after no long time I noticed that I had become the observed of all observers, namely a rabblement of children gathering brushwood, so I returned to decorum and proceeded soberly upon the highway. Through quaint hamlets and snug crofts I came down to the euphonious and picturesque village of Rocca Pietore, where for a very few centesimi I bought a vast number of cherries. The children regarded me at first with a certain awe, due to the badge on my Athletic Union blazer, but when I commenced a largesse of cherries, they began to gambol and hop around me, like the birds about St Francis. As I majestically stalked out of the township I was followed by a multitude of brats of various sizes, like the Piper of Hamelin's rats;—dolichocephalous brats eyed like the gentian that blooms by the peat-pool, brown-headed brats with eyes like the peat-pool itself, sturdy brats tottering at my side, and chubby little brats trotting along at their sisters' skirts. Jolly "bambini" they were, though of course they did talk too fast. They asked if I came from "Inghilterra," and when I replied with severe exactitude "Scozia," they were vastly dumbfounded, as if I had said Ruritania or Niffelheim. At last the little legs tired of keeping up with my rather long ones, and I descended solitary into Caprile, at a time when all sensible people were already recumbent in the shade. But cherries are unbulky fodder and importunate hunger was urging. In the heat of the day I staggered into a shady "Albergo," and devoured, under the mild and fiery glances respectively of the King and the Ruler of Italy, a vast number of omelettes, cunningly devised by the stout "Padrona" with subtle-flavoured herbs of the mountains, not without the cheerful juice of Terlano. And I heartily concurred in the sentiment of the gentle Mantuan:

"Quid juvat aestivo defessum pulvere abesse,
nec potius bibulo decubuisse toro?"

"Milia tum pransi tria repimus," up a cork-screw path on a wooded hillside, where vipers bask on the rocks and lizards drowse in the shade and only the cicadas interrupt the warm silences of the glades.

"Nunc cantu crebro rumpunt arbusta cicadae,
nunc vepris in gelida sede lacerta latet."

Then down I sit among the red-boled pines, where the ants scurry about; and dip into a little Greek book, and more often into a bag of cherries; and gaze round upon the marvellous peaks of the Dolomites, Marmolata's glistening snows and Monte Civetta's diademed head pondering over the bright lake of Alleghe.

Under that tranquil expanse of pale emerald and flashing sapphire lie buried four villages of men. It was a day in mid-winter of 1771 when a charcoal-burner came running down from the craggy slopes of Mount Forca, and cried through all the villages about its base, "The mountain is moving!" "Impossible," replied the good folk, "Never has it moved before, why should it move now?" And they retired to sleep in all confidence. Then in the dead of night the whole mountain-side came tumbling down and crushed two of the villages, with all their good folk asleep, and the stalled cows, and the little pink pigs in the orchards. And the debris piled itself high in the valley-bottom, so that the rushing river Cordevole was pent back and rose up and overwhelmed the two villages on its banks, and neither man nor beast escaped drowning. To-day a veil of trees and mosses and shrubs and little flowering plants is swathed about the broken side of the mountain, but high up on its face is stretched a gaunt line of precipices like an unhealed wound, to remind us of the sudden ruin of four villages of men, and the making of that calm and tranquil lake.

And now I attain the hill-crest, and the magnificence of Monte Pelmo bursts upon the view,—a veritable royalty, seated on a throne whereof the steps are terraces of eternal ice, and the sides sheer precipices of hideous depth.

At Villagrande I fill my ruck-sack with lumps of bread and cheese and chocolate, and inquire concerning my further path. "The Signor wishes to sleep on the Alto Nuvolau to see the sun rise. Santa Croce! It is not to be thought of. He will be frozen to death. And if he wishes to reach Cortina d'Ampezzo, surely the high-road of the Government is speedier?" However the mad Inglese does not change his mind. "Signor, there are many evil quarry-labourers on the mountain." "Are the valley-dwellers then so exemplary?" "But, Signor, it is three hours' walking, and the sun will set in two." Thereupon I produced my sleeping-bag, to the amazement of the good peasant, who doubtless regarded it as some kind of magic carpet to waft me through the leagues of air, and off I strode.

Then up through the pine-woods, on a rough cobbled track of immemorial age, whereby for thousands of years the peasants of the Val di Codalunga have brought down their tilted sledges of scented hay; I emerged upon the high downs of scanty turf, pink and red with azalea and rhododendron, and dotted over with the quaint log-barns, in one of which I proposed to pass the night. I met with the quarry-labourers, who were far from evil,—very friendly fellows, on the contrary, singing to a concertina as they sat at supper before the doors of the huts, while the sun set flaring over the ocean of mountains. With eloquent shruggings of the shoulders they watched the mad Inglese stalking on along the ridge, and heartily cried out "A rividerla!", for they thought I would come back to their huts in no time. But I found quite an eligible and exclusive chamber for the night in a hut by a little stream that served at once for refreshment and ablution. There was a bundle of fresh hay and not too great a smell of cows. So I supped and wrapped myself up in my sleeping-sack,—believe it or not, in that genteel and civilised garment, silk pyjamas—and swiftly fell asleep.

That was about ten o'clock, and shortly after four I awoke, as warm as a pie for the most part, but somewhat clammy as to the face, for a dank mist had invaded the hut, and much rain had dripped through the roof. After breakfasting on bread and cheese and icy water, I arose and girded on my ruck-sack and ventured forth into the outer chill. There was a rolling sea of mist in every direction, and it was exceedingly cold, for I was upwards of 7,000 feet above the sea. My utmost range of vision was ten yards, so that my hopes of viewing the Dawn on the Dolomites had evaporated. I therefore decided to adopt the quickest means of ministering to my creature comforts, and set off at a rapid pace over the rocky saddle whereby led the way to hot coffee and a hot bath.

It was eerie in that pale and uniform light, for I had no shadow to keep me company, and if I sang the surrounding blanket of mist echoed back a most mournful noise. I wandered among dripping black rocks and glistening white snow-drifts. By the path grew Aethionemas, their brilliant colours ashy grey in that dim twilight, and cheerful golden buttercups of startling size, and the fringed bells of Soldanellas and myriads of little white crocuses that sprout up directly the snow melts. With these for company I descended from the rocky saddle and over the moors of anemones and gentians and through pine-woods with columbines and campanulas; and now and again the mists would drift apart and reveal for a moment some giant of the Dolomites bathed in the early radiance; and at last as I came to the last ridge overlooking Cortina, the sun finally conquered, the mists flew away, and there lay before my hungry gaze that highly cosmopolitan resort with its elegant campanile, and the soft and varied charm of the Val d'Ampezzo ringed round with ferocious peaks, and the marvellous pinnacles and glaciers of Monte Cristallo.

So I came, like Odysseus to the palace of Alkinoos, to a palatial hotel, and lounged in an ample bath with every sort of complicated gadget, and retired to a luxurious bed, and received many cordial beverages from the hand of another Nausikaa. And Nausikaa observed with a charming smile, "Of course, you English are incredibly foolish, walking about in such rough places. We Italians much prefer to drive in a motor-car."

From *Auntran Blads*

*Published by William MacLellan, Glasgow, 1943, and dedicated
to the Gaelic poets Sorley Maclean and George Campbell Hay*

George Hay was a contemporary at Oxford and Douglas and he
planned to publish in 1939 a joint volume of verse which had been
approved by Edwin Muir, following the example of Robert Garioch
and Sorley Maclean who had issued such a volume, *17 Poems for
Sixpence*, in 1940. War conditions prevented this but Douglas
continued to write verses at odd times as incidents and states of
feeling suggested them. These were published as *Auntran Blads*.

The third quoted is a translation of Hay. The fifth was inspired
by him associated with the title of Maurice O'Sullivan's story of
life on the Blasket Islands, *Twenty Years A-growing*.

YE WERE THE DAWN

Frae the Gaelic o Sorley Maclean (Dàin do Eimhir LIV)

Ye were the dawn on the hills o the Cuillin,
the bousum day on the Clarach arisan,
the sun on his elbucks i the gowden flume,
the whyte rose-fleur that braks the horizon.

Gesserant sails on a skinklan frith,
gowd-yalla luft and blue o the sea . . .
the fresh mornan in your heid o hair
and your clear face wi its bonnie blee.

Gowdie, my gowdie o dawn and the derk
your loesome gentrice, your brou sae rare . . .
albeid wi the dullyart stang o dule
the breist o youth's been thirlit sair.

MY EEN ARE NAE ON CALVARY

Frae the Gaelic o Sorley Maclean

My een are nae on Calvary
or the Bethlehem they praise,
but on the shitten back-lands in Glesga toun
whaur growan life decays,
and a stairheid room in an Embro land,
a chalmer o puirtith and skaith,
whaur monie a shilpet bairnikie
gaes smoorit doun til daith.

THONDER THEY LIGG

"Thonder they ligg on the grund o the sea,
nae the hyne whaur they wald be."
Siccan a thing has happenit me
sin my son's been gane. When he was wee
I dannlit the bairn like a whelpikie
and he leuch i ma airms richt cantilie.
It's the auld weird nou I maun dree.

The luft grows derk, the sun gangs laigh,
atuor the skerries the sea-maws skreigh,
the rowtan kye come schauchlan doun,
the laddies rant out-throu the toun;
but here I rock at the fire ma lane,
mindan o him I had that's gane.

I see your jacket on the heuk,
but the hous islown in ilka neuk,
never a sound r a word i the room,
nae sclaffan o buits on the threshart-stane,
the bed cauld and the chalmer toom.

Gin it's the sych that traivels far
ye'll hear my sychan whaur ye are,
sleepan i the wrack, jundied aye,
wi ugsome felies sooman by,
the ghaistlie monsters o the sea.

"Wheesht, woman, wheesht, and deavena me.
My wae's the mair to see ye greet.
The ship brak doun under our feet,
life gaed aff, and memorie wi 't.
London slew me, weary faa 't,
connacht the een that never saw it.
Aiblins I was acquent wi you,
the saut has reingeit my memorie nou.

Here I stravaig i the merchless faem,
yestreen Donald was my name.
The wecht o your wae liggs sair on me.
Woman, wheesht, whae'er ye be."

Sair the price maun be dounpitten
by the island-fowk for the greatness o Britain.

hyne, haven; *sych*, sigh; *jundied*, rocked, jostled; *reinge*, scour;
stravaig, wander; *merchless*, unbounded.

FOR ALASDAIR

Written while fishing on the banks of the Calder at Lochwinnoch
in 1941, in memory of a Highland student at Aberdeen, killed
during the German advance into Libya.

Standan here on a fogg-yirdit stane,
drappan the bricht flees on the broun spate,
I'm thinkan o ye, liggan thonder your lane,
i the het Libyan sand, cauld and quate.
        The spate rins drumlie and broun,
        whummlan aathing doun.

The fowk about Inverness and Auld Aberdeen
aye likeit ye weel, for a wyce and a bonny man.
Ye were gleg at the Greekan o't, and unco keen
at gowf and the lave. Nou deid i the Libyan sand.
  The spate rins drumlie and broun,
  whummlan aathing doun.

Hauldan the Germans awa frae the Suez Canal,
ye dee'd. Suld this be Scotland's pride, or shame?
Siccar it is, your gallant kindly saul
maun lea thon land and tak the laigh road hame.
  The spate rins drumlie and broun,
  whummlan aathing doun.

fogg-yirdit, moss-covered; *the laigh road*, by which the dead travel, very speedily.
"Ye'll tak the high road and I'll tak the low road, and I'll be in Scotland afore ye."

FOR THE OLD HIGHLANDS

That old lonely lovely way of living
in Highland places,—twenty years a-growing,
twenty years flowering, twenty years declining,—
father to son, mother to daughter giving
ripe tradition; peaceful bounty flowing;
one harmony all tones of life combining,—
old wise ways, passed like the dust blowing.

That harmony of folk and land is shattered,—
the yearly rhythm of things, the social graces,
peat-fire and music, candle-light and kindness.
Now they are gone it seems they never mattered,
much, to the world, those proud and violent races,
clansmen, and chiefs whose passioned greed and blindness
made desolate these lovely lonely places.

42

WINTER HOMILY ON THE CALTON HILL

These chill pillars of fluted stone
shine back the lustre of the leaden sky,
stiff columns clustered on a dolerite hill
in solemn order, an unperfected vision
dimly gleaming. Not at random thrown
like old Greek temples that abandoned lie
with earthquake-riven drums. Rigid and chill
this still-born ruin stands for our derision.

A fine fantasy of the Whig literati
to build a modern Athens in our frore islands,
those elegant oligarchs of the Regency period,
Philhellenic nabobs and the Scots nobility.
As soon expect to meet a bearded Gujerati
stravaiging in a kilt throu the uttermost Highlands,
or in Princes Street gardens a coy and blushing Nereid.
Athens proved incapable of such mobility.

Is the thing meaningless, as it is astonishing,
a senseless fantasy, out of time and place?
Apeing foreign fashions is always derisible,
and mimicry, for Plato, was the soul's unmaking.
The ruin is symbolic, a symbol admonishing
Scottish posterity. Seekers after grace
must not imitate the outward and visible.
The culture of Athens was a nation's awaking.

EPILOGUE TO THEOKRITOS

I dinna ken the sense o ma trauchlan
owresettan thochts frae a by-gane leid
nou that amang the ruins of Europe
me and my students micht sune be deid.

Is it time tint threepan Theokritos
at the King's College in Aberdeen

43

to thir twa lasses and seeven callants
wi their scrabblan pens and their bricht een?

Whiles they're gleg and whiles dozent,
I crack my jokes to mak them gay,
but I dout a wheen o us 'll sune be lauchan
wi ither fowk's chafts, as the Greeks say.

What matter a syncopate second aorist
or a variant lection in manuscript C,
Arsinoe's tableau or Simaitha's havers,
when Daith bydes on us momentlie?

Instans tyrannus. . . . But och, why fash
for the waesome war, that doesna inspire us,
nae me oniewey, wi onie rowth o pleasure?
As weel warssle wi the Antinoe papyrus.

The first stanza is a metapoiesis of Sorley Maclean's Dain do Eimhir, LV.
chafts, jaws (cf. "laugh on the other side of one's face").

SANG BY THE SEA

Nae bore o blue i the lither lyft,
nae gair o blue i the dullyart sea;
eerie and dreich the cluds drift,
dreich and eerie the swaws shift,
and me dowf as a chiel can be.

C'wa, lass, and turn your een on me,
the wints o your een that are bonny blue,
lauchan wi a leam like sun on the sea
fraemang your face's sunbrunt blee,
the twa lauchan starnies I loe.

bore, patch, gap; *lither*, undulating with dim clouds; *wints*, pupils.

44

FIFE EQUINOX

*Written in 1939 around lines 9 and 10 which he heard
actually uttered by a servant girl at Ardlogie.*

Ae day and ae nicht a yowden-druft
fae the cauld nor-aist has whusslit and pufft
and blawn the craws about the luft,
blatteran sairlie;
it reeshlit the wuids and gart them shuft
like a breer o barley.

The cypress-busses are aa blawn cruikit,
the greens are as clorty as onie doocot;
the wind-faan epples 'll hae to be cuikit
afore they get waur.
The plooms are aa wersh, they're that sair droukit
and clortit wi glaur.

yowden-druft, downwards driving rain-storm; *clortit*, filthied.

WHILES

It's nae juist canny, whiles, readan Plato
or onie ither buik
a young man's een see twa ither een
wi a glamarie luik,
sae's he canna tak tent
what auld Plato meant
for thir een and their glent.

An orra thing tae, at Ochrida or onie place
whaur there's a loch
whiles ye see i the faem o the swaw
a shouther or hough,
sae's ye'd aamaist swear
a lass sooms there
i thon gesserant gair.

45

Ye ken it's by-ordinar, at Sveti Naüm
or in onie skug
whaur fullyerie reeshles, whiles a voice
rouns i your lug
couthy and saft
wi an auntran waft
sae's ye think ye're daft.

Sveti Naüm, monastery near Ohrid in Serb Macedonia;
gesserant gair, sparkling patch; *rouns*, whispers; *auntran*, occasional.

SABBATH I THE MEARNS

The geans are fleuran whyte i the green Howe o the Mearns;
wastlan winds are blawan owre the Mownth's cauld glacks,
whaur the whaups wheep round their nesties amang the fog and ferns;
and the ferm-touns stand gray and lown, ilk wi its yalla stacks.
The kirk is skailan, and the fowk in Sabbath stand o blacks
are doucely haudan hame til their denners wi the bairns,
the young anes daffan and auld neebours haean cracks.

Thon's bien and canty livan for auld-farrant fermer-fowk
wha wark their lives out on the land, the bonnie Laigh o Mearns.
They pleu and harra, saw and reap, clatt neeps and tattie-howk,
and dinna muckle fash theirsels wi ither fowks' concerns.
There's whiles a chyld that's unco wild, but sune the wildest learns
gin ye're nae a mensefu fermer-chiel ye's be naething but a gowk,
and the auld weys are siccar, auld and siccar like the sterns.

They werena aye like thon, this auld Albannach race,
whas stanes stand heich upo the Mownth whaur the wild whaup caas.
Focht for libertie wi Wallace, luikit tyrants i the face,
stuid a siege wi leal Ogilvie for Scotland's king and laws,
i the Whigs' Vaut o Dunnottar testifeed for Freedom's cause.
Is there onie Hope to equal the Memories o this place?
The last Yerl Marischal's deid, faan doun his castle waas.

glacks, passes; *clatt*, hoe; *mensefu*, moderate, well-behaved; Sir George Ogilvie of Barras held Dunnottar Castle, with Charles II's regalia inside, against the Cromwellian General Monck.

ON THE AKROPOLIS AT SKOPLJE, JULY 1936

Here on the hillside garden the dusk closes;
elderly gardeners shuffle about, watering
green graves of old Turkish pashas among the roses,—
bones and dust after their lust and slaughtering.

Down there in the vaporous street the crowds are strolling
in the evening coolness; a brass band booming and battering
blares on the square by the bridge, where elegant officers lolling
with their would-be Parisian dames are sipping and whiffing and chattering.

With long red fingers caressing, the bright day leaves
that stark fortress piled on its swart precipice,
where Serbian serfs skewered the veal and bay-leaves
for epicure pashas, wise in delicate recipes.

The pashas moulder, their vast empire vanished;
their Skoplje castle shelters a Serb garrison;
from the lands of their conquest the conquering race is banished.
(A wandering Scot gets pleasure from this comparison.)

The Shar Planina is pink now, the anonymous eastern highlands'
harsh dun contours flush with the hot sun's flattering.
The Vardar swirls amethystine round shimmering shingle islands
where the hooves of the cavalry rattle, Homerically clattering.

From the dim garden of the roses where the twilight glimmers
I see the men and the horses rush into the Vardar's eddying.
The floating manes of the horses and the flash of the splashing swimmers
kindle a tingling excitement that is quite unsteadying.

I must go down from this hill and swim in the swirling Vardar,
Homer's "fair-eddying Axios." Leaving the modern, habitual,
aesthetic, neurotic perhaps, I must seek the older and harder
barbarous primitivity, the swimmer's strengthening ritual.

It is three thousand years from Homer to me, his scholar,
who read him on India paper, an aesthetical Oxonian,

in my grey linen trousers and coat, my shirt and my tie and my collar,
him with his wreath and his lyre, a trailing-tunicked Ionian.

But if he were here now, looking down from this hillside garden,
we would both have the same excitement, the heart heavily battering,
the urge to strip and to plunge in the waters that soothe and harden,
to race and shout on the shingle to the rhythm of the hard hooves' clattering.

Shar Planina, main range of Macedonia.

On May 10, 1940 Hitler invaded the Low Countries and on reading
the report in *The Times* next day Douglas wrote the next three
poems straight off in sequence. The second is in sprung rhythm
imitating the metre of *Piers Plowman*. The third harks back to an
incident ten years previously but influenced by a Dracula film he
had seen.

SPECULATION

Gin the firmament was nearer
or the lyft whiles clearer
wald we ken the starns mair certainlie, or less?

Aiblins the universalitie
and unco mathematicalitie
o Astronomie's naebut kenners' pretentiousness.

The wey it is wi men
it's the masses that we ken,
but never ae man kens anither's consciousness.

And why suldna the starns
hae ilk their ain harns
and sclents o their ain that we dinna see wi the gless?

harns, brains; *sclents*, inclinations.

48

THE CAT IN THE ROCK-GARDEN

Ha! the blue trumpets blowing triumphantly,
brilliant, gem-like, blooms of gentian,
and yellow hoop-petticoats poising prettily,
where the white puss wonderingly wanders.

Look! she's away, the white tail waving,
archly bounding on the brown andesite,
red-brown rocks where aubrietias cataract,
pale purple, pink, vivid violet.

Now she pauses and poses a paw
at a flaunting tulip from far Turkmenistan,
Sniffs the pink daphne from Dolomite screes,
peers in the pool at her own white whiskers,

AUGUST NIGHT

What is thatt? What iz it? Swish-swishing about me in the dark,
fluttering and twittering in the hot empty night?
God! I'm sweating, my heart thumps, thumps, and a stark
terror bristles my hair. Christ! let me put on the light.
Hell! It's dazzling, I can't see, it's hellishly bright.
My glasses. Ah, that's better. It's only a bat.
It can't hurt. No need to be in such a fright.
I don't care, I'm going to kill him. I'll squash him flat.

So I got up and took a towel and began swiping crazily
at the maddening creature, and the light swayed dizzily,
and the curtains flapped and the papers on the table fluttered
and the bat flew frantically about and shrilly twittered,
and I sweated and swore and got nearly hysterical,
swiped . . . missed . . . swiped . . . missed . . . and at last by a miracle hit him.

He fell on a shelf, on Farnéll's Pindar,
volume III, and clung a second. I was struck with wonder
at his gleaming eyes and his silk-and-velvety softness.

Then he fell on the rug, dead. With hideous swiftness
the lustre faded off. I felt myself a criminal
when I saw calmly the dusty corpse of the frail animal.
Out of the window I threw it with a shuddering horror,
and ran to wash my hands, and there in the mirror
saw my face, and was shocked at my own terror.

A LOVE

It came unsought for, undesired,
and left me unregretted.
A day or two my soul was fired,
but dwindling soon that flame expired,
and my dirige was "Let it."
I'd sooner lie calm and cool.
Why trouble to boil a stagnant pool?

ARDLOGIE, CHRISTMAS EVE, 1939

The mild midwinter evening ebbs, leaving
wreckage of gold and purple on the hill.
The full round moon sails up from eastward, cleaving
dim veils of star-split cloud, tenuous and still.

Winter has jewels yet, leaf, flower, and berry,
berberis, holly, crab, and many more;
wych-hazels' golden straps, a starry cherry,
primroses, heaths, a purple hellebore.

There's a viburnum by the porch, some vagrant
botanist found in western Yunnan.
It's flowering now, exquisitely fragrant,
waxy white umbels, scent of marzipan.

Moon-white the naked beeches tower, wreathing
lichened limbs above the laurel glooms;
beyond the lawn a ground-air faintly breathing
stirs the white torches of the pampas plumes.

About me as I walk an odour lingers
of cypress logs I sawed; the pungent scent
clings in my tweeds, and when I raise my fingers
I get the resinous smell, and am content.

Cock-pheasants from the neighbouring pinewood chortle,
a blackbird whistles from the red-twigged lime,
There's enough pleasure here for any mortal
with eyes, ears, nose, this mild midwinter-time.

EIRINN AG GUL
(IRELAND GREITAN)
Frae the Scots Gaelic o William Livingstone

Uttermost isle of Europe
loveliest land under sky,
often I saw your coastline
beyond ocean's bellowing cry.

With the south-east blowing gently
and in heaven no mist or cloud
the Gaels in the Rhinns of Islay
admired your beauty aloud.

THON TIME WE AA WONNED
Frae the Aiolic o Psappho

Thon time we aa wonned thegither,
she was shair o ye then, and worshippt ye neist;
she loed your singan abune aa ither.

Braw amang Lydian leddies nou
she gaes, like the rose-fingert mune
wi aa the starns about her brou,

eftir the sun's doungangan. The leam
streiks out on the monie-fleurit hauchs
and kelters owre the saut sea's stream.

51

Doun draps the dauch in a bonnie shouer,
roses blaw rowthie, and saft chervil,
and the hinnie-sawrit clover-fleur.

Stravaigan aften her lane she'll gae,
thinkan lang til her gentie Atthis,
forfant in spreit, and her hert wae.

wonned, dwelt; *dauch*, dew; *hinnie-sawrit*, honey-smelling;
thinkan lang til, yearning for; *forfant*, faint, enfeebled.

TIL ANAKTORIA

Frae the Aiolic o Psappho

Maik o the gods he seems to me,
thon man that sits in front o ye,
and hears your talkan couthilie near,
sae saftlie and clear,

your luvelie lauchan. My hert stounds
rowsan i ma breist when your lauch sounds,
and gif I glent at ye sittan there
I canna speak mair.

Ma tung freezes i ma mou, a nesh
lowe rins chitteran throu ma flesh;
nae sicht i ma een; wi their nain thunner
ma lugs dunner.

Swyte reems doun me; frae heid to fuit
a trummlan grups me, sae's I sit
greener nor gerss, in sic a dwalm
I kenna wha I am.

Maik, mate; *nesh*, delicate.

FOWR EPIGRAMS FRAE THEOGNIS O MEGARA

I've been a gangrel bodie, I've been to Sicilie,
and owre til Euboia wi the vines upon its howe,
bonnie Sparta on Eurotas whaur the rashes grow.
And aa the fowk in ilka place were guid to me.
But I'd nae rowth o pleasure for aa that I micht see.
Och, I'd suner be at hame in ma ain countrie.

They pledge me nae mair in wine, for nou anither,
far waur nor me, courts ma dentie lassie.
In cauld watter they curse me, her faither and mither.
Aye greetan for me she rins to fill the tassie
at the well, whaur yince wi ma airm about her back
I kisst her halse, and saftlie her mou spak.

Yill's ma guid frien, but ae thing that's agee,—
when I get fechtan-fou and meet wi ma enemie.
But gin it flees to ma heid and winna byde i ma wame,
och, then I gie owre the yill and gae awa hame.

Drinkan, I heedna puirtith that eats the hert,
or the clash o ill-deedie men that wad mak me smert;
but I'm wae for ma luvely virr that desarts me nou,
and I greet for auld age coman, that gars me grue.

HEKTOR'S TWYNAN FRAE ANDROMACHA
Frae Homer's Iliad, VI, 392-496

Syne when he cam to the Skaian yetts as he gaed throu the burgh,
whaur he beguid to gae under the port on his wey to the howe-land, there
his weel-tochert wife Andromacha cam til him rinnan, King Eetion's
dochter that was, great-hertit and namely, auld Eetion's sel, that wonned
in weel-wuidit Plakos, under Ben Plakos in Thebe, Cilician fowk was his
people; his ae dochter it was that was marriet on Hektor the bress-graitht.
Thon time she cam to meet him. A hous-queyn followit eftir, haudan
the bairn til her breist, juist a wee bit tapitless bairnie, Hektor's bairn that
he loed, that was bonny as ane o the starnies. Hektor wald caa him Skam-

andrios aye, but Astyanax maistlie aabody nemmt him. Alane it was
Hektor was sauvan the citie (*note 1*).

Lauchanlie then he luikt at his bairn, luikt lauchan, but spakna;
standan aside him the wife Andromacha grat, and wi greitan gruppit his
haund and caad him by name and spak til him, sabban:

"Fey that ye are, your micht'll be daith til ye. Never your bairnie tak
ye thocht til ava, or your wifikie, me that'll sune be widdawt o ye. The
Achaians aiblins 'll sune hae ye slauchtert, aa rinnan on ye at yince. And
me, gif e'er I suld tine ye, better for me to gae under the yirth. For never
anither solace I'll ken, quhan ye sall dree your weird that is weirdit, naething but dule. Nae faither I hae, or leddie my mither. Na, na. Lang syne
faither was slauchtert by godlike Achilles, him that herriet the thraipfu
broch o the fowk o Cilicie, Thebe o heich-biggit ports, and Eetion's sel he
dounharlit. Ruvena the graith o him tho, but respectit him out o his
honour, brunt his corp on a pyre wi his wappens bonnilie round him,
biggit a cairn til him tae. The nymphs that wone i the hielants plantit elms
around it, the dochters o Zeus wi the aigis.

"Ay, and at hame thon time I had seeven brether about me. Och, but
the hale o them gaed thon ilk ae day doun til Hades. Aa in ae tulyie he
slew, the fieryfit godlike Achilles, there wi their schauchlan kye and the
yowes wi the kenspeckle flesches. Mither forbye, that was queen, owre
thonder by weel-wuidit Plakos, her he brocht here thon time wi the lave o
the gear that he herriet, syne let her gae awa hame for a ransoun fairlie
past countan. Doun in her faither's haa it was archeress Artemis strack her,
"Hektor, ye nou alane are my faither and matronlie mither, ye are my
brither alane, forbye the braw lad that I bed wi. Come awa cannilie nou.
tak tent, and byde on the touer, makna your bairn an orpheling-wean and
your wifie a widdaw. Battle your fowk til the fecht at the fig-tree, whaur
they micht spiel up aisiest intil the broch, and rin in whaur the waa has
been thirlit. Thrice dounby they assayt an onfaa wi the wale o their
fechters, round thae twa they caa Aias and kenspeckle Idomeneeus, round
the twa sons o king Atreus and Tydeus' feerichan laddie. Aiblins a chiel
wi the second-sicht had gien them a tellan, aiblins they lippent i thochts o
their ain and canny devysans."

Syne muckle Hektor answerit her, wi his bassanat skinklan: "Wife,
it's me 'll tak tent til aa thon. But I'm fairly affrichtit what 'll be said by
the menfowk o Troy and the lang-skirtit weemen, howdrand awa gin I
byde like a smeddumless cuif frae the battle. Na, my hert says me na. I
was gleg aye to be wurdy, foremaist aye i the fechtan amang the prime o

the Troymen, winnan renoun to ma faither and meikle renoun to ma nyawn sel. Weel I ken this i ma hert, and my ingyne tells it me trulie: Tyde sall betyde quhan Ilios toun that is haly sall periss, Priam tae and the fowk o king Priam, guid wi the ash-spear. Less, for aa that, am I fasht by thon dule o the Trojans ahint me (*note 2*), neitherans Hekabe's dule, that's ma mither, or dule o king Priam, neither ma brithers' weird, that for aa they are mony and bonnie doun sall faa i the stour and dee at the hands o their faemen,—less for aa thir nor for thee, quhan some bress-sarkit Achaian luggs ye greitan awa, takan frae ye the day o your freedom. Thonder in Argos syne ye'll tent the loom til anither, rin to the well in Messeis aiblins or far Hypereia, sair and aften affrontit, a strang lourd weird 'll be on ye. Aiblins a body 'll say, that sees ye greitan fou sairlie: 'Thon yin's Hektor's wife, him that aye was the wale o the fechters, Troyland's bauld chevaliers, quhan for Ilios toun they did battle.' Siclike aiblins they'll say, and a new dule then 'll be on ye, want o a man like me to keep aff ye the seasoun o thralldom. God, quhan I'm deid, i the murlit mools I'd wuss to be yirdit or I suld hear your skreigh o distress and your waeful mischievan."

Sae spak gesserant Hektor, and raxt out his hand til his bairnie. Och, but the wean outskraugh, sclentan back on the breist o his nourrice, fairlie dumbfoundert he was at the sicht o his daddie that loed him, fleggit sair at the bress and the crest wi its wallopan horsehair, kelteran doun frae the tap o the bassanat, unco the sicht o't.

Lang then the baith o them leuch, his dad and the ladie his mither. Syne the begesserant Hektor releaseit his bree frae the helmonte, dounpit it then on the broun derk yird, whaur it bonnilie skinklit. Kissan the bairn that he loed and dandlan 't a wee in his arms, spak he a prayer richt herty to Zeus and the lave o the godheids:

"Zeus and aa ither gods, let this bairnikie be like ma ain sel, virrfu like me in his micht and the maister o Ilios burgh. Syne may somebody say 'He's better a sicht nor his faither,' quhan he comes up frae the war. May he come wi wappens aa bluidie, graith o a fae he's slain, and the hert o his mither be blythened."

Siclike spak he, and neist gya back his son til his wifie, intil her hend that he loed. At her breist she happit him saftlie, lauchan and greitan at yince. And her man was routh at the sicht o't, straikit her then wi's hand and spak til her couthie and hertlie:

"Hinnie, dinna be fasht owre sairlie for me i your spreit nou. Nae man 'll send me to Hell gin it's nae the time that is weirdit. Nae man, trulie

I tell ye, sall flee frae his weird that is weirdit, neither the cuif nor the guid man, the weird that is his frae his birth-tyde. Nou ye maun gang awa hame, and tak tent till your ain kind o jobbies, mirliego, loom, and the lave. And see that the lassies are eident tentan their wark. The war and the battle the men 'll tak tent til, me abune aa, and the lave that are bairnies o Ilios burgh."

Sae spak gesserant Hektor, and liftit the bassanat blythlie, horse-hair-crestit and aa; and his dear wife gaed awa hamewith, turnan aften to luik at her man, aye greitan fou sairlie.

Note 1: Skamandros is ane o the meikle flumes o the Trojan howe. Astyanax, "Maister of the broch," a by-name gien til the bairn out o honour til his faither.
Note 2: the Greeks had a notion o gaean backward intil the time coman, the Gaels o gaean uphill.
tapitless, heedless; *thraipfu,* prosperous; *aigis,* shield o the god; *flesches,* fleeces; *bassanat,* helmet; *begesserant,* glittering; *mirliego,* spindle; *eident,* diligent.

LASSIE, C'WA

Frae Catullus, V. "Vivamus, mea Lesbia, atque amemus . . ."

Lassie, c'wa, let 's live in houghmagandie.
The life o luve 's the life for you and me.
Gif unco-guid Kirk-Elders caa us randy
we'll fashna for their snash but ae bawbee.
Suns can gae doun and rise as bonnilie,
but us,—when yince-for-aa our wee bit licht
gaes doun, we're hapt for aye in ae lang nicht.

I LOED YE YINCE

Frae the Russin o Pushkin

I loed ye yince, and aiblins i ma hert
thon luve 's nae aathegither dwineit awa.
But dinna let it fash ye onie mair,
I waldna seek to gar ye greet ava.
I loed ye tungless, loed ye hopelesslie,
whiles unco jalous, whiles owre blate to woo ye.
I loed ye yince, saw tenderlie, sae trulie,
as gie 't ye God some ither chiel may loe ye.

56

Ich liebte dich. Mag sein dass jene Liebe
brennt noch und funkelt mir in diesem Herz.
Doch huet' Du dich vor jedem traur'gen Triebe,
ich moechte wohl dir machen keinen Schmerz.
Ich liebte dich ganz hoffnungslos, verschwiegen,
durch Eifersucht gequaelt, und sonst durch Scheu.
Dir treu und zart all' mein' Gedanken stiegen.
Gott geb dir einen ander'n Mann so treu.

    Aiolic, eftir Psappho:

      Αἰολιστί.

Ἠράμαν μὲν ἔγω σέθεν, Ἄτθι, πάλαι ποτά,
καρδία δ' ἐν ἴσως ἔτι μοι φλέγεται πόθα.
ἀλλὰ μή τι πάθῃς· στυγέραις ὀνίαις σέθεν γ'
    εὔχομ' ἄπεμμεν·

ἠράμαν ποτ' ἄναυδος ἄνελπις· ἐτρυχόμαν
αἴδοι ζαλοσύνᾳ τ'· ἀδόλως μάλα μολθάκως τ'
ἠράμαν ἔρον οἶον ἔχην ποτά σοι Κύπρις
    δοίη ὔπ' ἄλλῳ.

THOUGHT FOR ST ANDREW'S NIGHT, 1936

    I wish I were a crocodile
    to haunt the muddy streams of Nile
    and nibble niggers' toes.
    I'd bask upon a sunny bank,
    eat virgins of the highest rank,
    and vomit up their cloes.

    Caenosas utinam natare possem
    Aegypti crocodilus inter undas;
    morderem Aethiopum pedes nigellos,
    apricae volutans vadis harenae
    queis gens optima virgines comessem;
    rursus prospuerem venusta Coa.

Εὐριπιδαριστοφανιστί.

Εἴθε γενοίμην κροκόδειλός τις
Νείλου ἐπ᾽ ὄχθαις πηλοτρόφοισιν·
εἴθ᾽ ἐμπλήμην Μαυρῶν ποδίων,
ἡλίου αὐγαῖς θερμαινόμενος,
μεγάλων τε δόμων θυγατέρας ἐδόμενος,
εἶτα καλὴν ἐσθῆτ᾽ ἐμέσων.

(*to a René Clair sort of tune*)
Si j'étais un beau crocodile
pour me rouler sous la boue du Nil,
mordre les doigts des nègres indigènes,
me coucher sur rives remplies de soleil,
dévorer les filles du meilleur degré,—
je vomirais leurs vêtements sans beaucoup de peine.

To an early XIXth century German ballad-type tune

Ich moechte ein Krokodil werden,
das gluecklichste Tier auf Erden,
wohl bei dem stroemenden Nil;
er wohnt im warmen Wasser,
da findest du nichts nasser,
und lebt in grossartigem Stil.
und lebt in grossartigem Stil.

Gefuettert ist der Greis (ugh!)
mit Negern-fuesschen zur Speise;
er isst mit Schmaus und Braus.
Am sonnigen Ufer liegend,
seinen Riesen-ruecken umbiegend,
er haelt vorzuegliches Haus,
er haelt vorzuegliches Haus,

Maedleine von altem Adel,
auch schoen und ohne Tadel,
frisst er heruntergeschluckt;

58

die Kleider die sie tragen
aus seinem vollen Magen
sind wieder herausgespuckt,
bald wieder herausgespuckt.

FRAE THE LALLANS O BURNS "CAA THE YOWES"

Βοιωτιστί.

Βόσκε τὰς ἦγας τού νουν ἀν κολώνας,
δηῦτε πὸτ τὰν ἀνθεμόεντ' ἐρίκαν·
ἦγας ἐν κρωνὸν σουνέλα ῥίοντα,
νούμφα ποθεινά.

Σῖγα δ' αὐδὰν Ϝεσπερίαν κιχείλας
τάνδε πὲρ βάσσας ἀΐοισα Θίσβας
ἦγας ἐν σταθμὼς ταχέως ἔλα μοι,
νούμφα ποθεινά.

Πὰρ δὲ Περμεισσοῖ' ἀνίωμες ὄχθαν,
τᾶνδ' ἐν ἠγίρων σκιόεσσαν οὔλαν,
εἶ ῥιῖ δίνης οὐπὸ τὰν σελάναν
παμφανοώσης.

Ἄστου νοῦν μέττα 'Ωγούγιον σιωπᾶ
νουκτὶ Θίσβας, εἶ Χάριτες σελάνᾳ
τῦ χόρυ χήρονθι τά τ' ἄνθε' ἀδρᾷ
στίλβι ἐέρσᾳ.

Μεὶ φόβυ τεῖν Λαμίας ποκ' ἔντων
μειδὲ Μορμόος· τοὺ γὰρ 'Αφροδίτᾳ
φιλτάτα θιοῖσί τ' ἀδᾷος ἔσσῃ,
νούμφα ποθεινά.

'Αλλὰ καλά γ' ἔσσα, κόριλλ' ἐραννά,
στείθιος κάρδιαν κεκλόφωσ' ἔχις του·
τϲθνάνῃ 'στω, μϲίδ' ἀπολιμπάνην τίν,
νούμφα ποθεινά.

59

CARMEN IN PATRIAM SUAM

Melodiae aptum Abelardi "O quanta qualia
sunt illa sabbata"

S   Scotia, patria mea carissima,
terrarum omnium terra dulcissima,
de novo liberam te restituere
laetabor, hoc ego totus in opere.

C   Clara per secula tua progenies,
patrum nobilium filii nobiles,
nunquam sunt foediter passi servitium.
Libertas optimum omnibus premium.

O   Omnibus Calgaci, semper Valesii
cantetur gloria, Bruxisque splendidi.
Romanos invicem, Saxonas vicimus,
invicta natio unica fuimus.

T   Tot claris proavis nostri homunculi,
proh aetas degener, pravi miserrimi.
Scotorum cordibus quando praefervidum
ardebit pristinum illud ingenium?

I   Interim nostrum est mentes erigere,
et totis patriam votis appetere;
ad regnum Scotiam spreta Britannia
post longa regredi tandem exilia.

A   Ampla potentia, plena fecunditas
liberam te manent, summa felicitas.
Libertas sit tibi, paxque perpetua,
dilecta patria, usque per secula.

FRAE THE LALLANS O BURNS "AE FOND KISS"

Δωριστί.

Ὕστατον ἀμὲ φίλαμα μένει, χωρισμὸς ἔπεστι·
ἓν τόδε Χαῖρε λέγω, κὠδέποκ' αὖτις ἐρῶ.
δάκρυα δ' ἐκ βαθέος στέρνω προρίοντα προπίνων
τᾷ στάσει ἰυγμῶν καὶ στοναχᾶν μάχομαι.

Ἀλλὰ Τύχαν τίς ἐρεῖ δυσδαίμονα καὶ πολύκλαυστον
Ἐλπίδος ὄφρα κ' ἔχῃ τὸ σθένος ἀστέρος ὥς;
σμικροτάταν δ' οὔ πώ ποκ' ἐν ὠρανῷ ἔδρακον αἴλαν,
ἄχθος ἀμαυρὸν ἀεὶ κρύπτει ἀμαχανίας.

Οὐ τὸν πολλὸν ἔρωτα, τὸν ἄφρονα τόνδ', ὀνοτάζω.
Ἁλιοδώραν γὰρ πᾶς κεν ἰδὼν ἐμάνη·
εὐθὺς ἰδὼν ἐμάνη τε καὶ ἐς βαθὺν ἆλατ' ἔρωτα,
τάν τε φιλεῖ μώναν τάν τε φιλασεῖ ἀεί.

Αἰ 'πεφιλάμεθα νῶ γα πόθῳ μὴ τὼς μανιώδει,
αἰ 'μεμανάμεθα μὴ τυφλοτάτᾳ φιλίᾳ,
αἰ μή πώ ποχ' ὁμοῦ 'γεγενάμεθα, μή ποκα χωρίς,
οὔ κα νῦν ἄμφω τόσσον ἀθυμέομες.

Ἀλλὰ κορᾶν τὺ καλᾶν καλλίστα χαῖρε καὶ ἔμπας,
χαῖρε τὺ τὸν λοιπόν, φίλτατον ὄμμα, βίον.
Αἰὲς πᾶσα χάρις καὶ ἀγάλματα πάντα παρείη
χάρματά θ' Ἀσυχίας δωρά τε τᾶς Κύπριδος.

Ὕστατον ἦς τὸ φίλαμα τόδ' ἀμίν, μέσφα δ' ἐς αἰὲς
ἔρπωμες χωρὶς δάκρυσι καὶ στοναχαῖς.

61

From *Plastic Scots*

William MacLellan, Glasgow, 1946

THE REACTIONARY CARPINGS

From an address given to a meeting of the Dunedin Society in
Glasgow, Mr Hugh MacDiarmid in the chair. It is an account
and defence of the Lallans Movement.

IT IS AGAINST this interesting and hopeful movement that a considerable
volume of hostile comment has lately been directed, most notably in the
correspondence and other columns of *The Glasgow Herald* (November,
1946). May I briefly examine some of the criticisms?

I myself was signalled out for assault in the final editorial article con-
cluding the controversy (28th November), when Mr James Fergusson
wrote: "Those who have studied the correspondence and the writings of
Mr Douglas Young and his companions will hardly believe that the
language in which they claim that they naturally express themselves in
poetry bears other than the remotest relation to any form of Scots current
to-day." May I quote you a short piece of the writings mentioned, from
the Faber anthology of *Modern Scottish Poetry*:

> "The Minister said it wald dee,
>   the cypress-buss I plantit.
> But the buss grew til a tree,
>   naething dauntit.
> It's growan, stark and heich,
>   derk and straucht and sinister,
> kirkyairdie-like and dreich, ...
> But whaur's the Minister?"

I admit, to be sure, that the word *Minister* is a Latin word, and that
Dunbar and Henryson would have said *Priest*. I agree that *Cypress* is a
word derived through French from some pre-Hellenic *Minoan* tongue.
But I deny that these plastically amalgamated gobbets of language bear
not the remotest relation to any form of Scots current to-day. If that be so,
why should farmers on a market-day in Cupar poke me in the ribs and ask
Whaur's the Minister?

Among the anti-Renaissance diehards there is great complaint about the unintelligibility of neo-Lallans Makars. I remind them of Gawn Douglas's warning: "Weill at ane blenk slee poetry nocht tane is." In all cultured languages to-day some poets write some of their poems in words which are difficult to grasp because they are striving to communicate sensations and thoughts which are not commonly communicated and which are elusive and hard to express. If Blok and Rilke and T. S. Eliot and Paul Valéry are difficult in their own languages, even to persons well acquainted with Russian, German, English, and French, naturally they will remain difficult when translated into Lallans. Mr MacDiarmid and others have amply proved that even the greatest and hardest poets can be translated into Lallans, and it is worth the effort to understand them. A well-known English poet who is producing an anthology of versions from French, for which I had been asked to send pieces, recently wrote thanking me for a version I did in Lallans of Paul Valéry's *Le Cimitière Marin*, and commented:

> "Thank you for the lovely poem. Lacking Scots, as I do, even more than French, I was still able to enjoy much of it: and regret the lazy insularity of our public which hinders me from making use of so attractive a piece of work."

The true Scots were never insular or lazy, whatever may be said of our North-British critics.

A frequent allegation of the would-be critics is that the Renaissance Makars do not write as they speak, but read old books and dictionaries. Now no poet has ever written entirely as he or she spoke, not even Sappho, much less Wordsworth, who tried hard and flopped heavily. Still less has any poet written entirely as the common folk spoke. Proletarians in Stratford-on-Avon did not talk in the style of *"This hand would rather the multitudinous seas incarnadine,"* nor did Aeschylus' comrades-in-arms at Marathon converse after their victory in the diction of the choruses of his *Agamemnon.* All literary artists take from the colloquial speech about them, but they also take from their literary heritage, acquired by reading or recitation. If we were obliged to use no words we had not heard, we would be sadly restricted in our expressiveness. And as a source of expressions, a dictionary is quite as justifiable as any other book—if a good dictionary.

Another common indictment bears on the contemporary Makars' mixing of Scots dialects. I think myself each individual should adhere consistently, at any rate in any one piece, to the pronunciation of his own district, but it is legitimate to take words from any and every dialect, especially as the dialects have only emerged since the disintegration of King's Lallans after 1560.

A further accusation of a very heinous kind is that launched at our heads by Mr James Fergusson later in his editorial, that the Renaissance Makars are actuated mainly by a political motive, "a desire for as complete disassociation as possible from English speech and literary traditions." Now this allegation contains but a partial truth, for the Makars—I believe I can say all of them—share a desire to re-establish the cultural contacts of Lallans with other literatures which the English predominance had occluded, and to retrieve, refine, and extend Lallans as a national language fit for all purposes of verse, and indeed of literature generally. If in the pursuit of this aim some of them are more or less militantly anglophobe, that is a necessary result of the imperialist tendency of the English language in Scotland, claiming and by Act of Parliament securing a monopoly in schools and so forth. Continuing, Mr Fergusson wrote: "Apart from the impossibility of dividing cultures which have been for so long intertwined, this is a desire as mischievous as it is puerile." One recalls that not many years ago *The Glasgow Herald* had quite different comments to make on the Nazi policy of Germanisation in Poland and the resistance offered by cultured Poles to that aggression. One notes also an anti-Amurrican trend in the North and South British newspaper press, a wish to preserve the linguistic separateness of King's English as opposed to Uncle Sam's.

Taking refuge lastly in a patriotic note, Mr Fergusson opines that "It does no service to the Scottish people to try to seduce their literature into a jargon comprehensible to few in Scotland and to none but scholars any-where else." By contrast with this view of the Renaissance, one may con-sider the statement of the playwright James Bridie in *The Glasgow Herald* (14th November): "To recover and to weld together the scattered elements of the rich old Scottish language is surely not a contemptible enterprise." And Mr Eric Linklater, in a critical review of the Renaissance (*Poetry Scotland*, No. 3, p. 9) concludes: "Scotland has poets again and they are poets who put intellect in service to their passion, whose appetite is large, and their spirit high."

From *A Braird o Thristles*

Published by William MacLellan, Glasgow, 1947

Dedicated to his wife and containing several pieces already
printed in various periodicals.

FOR A WIFE IN JIZZEN

Lassie, can ye say
    whaur ye had been,
whaur ye had come frae,
    whatna ferlies seen?

Eftir the bluid and swyte,
    the warsslin o yestreen,
ye ligg forfochten, whyte,
    prouder nor onie queen.

Albeid ye hardly see me
    I read it i your een,
sae saft blue and dreamy,
    mindan whaur ye've been.

Anerly wives ken
    the ruits o joy and tene,
        the march o daith and birth,
            the tryst o luve and strife
i the howedumbdeidsunsheen,
    fire, air, water, yirth
        mellan to mak new life,
        lauchan and greetan, feiman and serene.

Dern frae aa men
    the ferlies ye ha seen.

ferlies, marvels; *warsslin*, wrestling, struggle; *ligg*, lie; *forfochten*, exhausted by struggle; *tene*, sorrow; *march*, boundary; *howedumbdeidsunsheen*, sunshine at dead of night; *mellan*, encountering; *lauchan*, laughing; *greetan*, crying; *feiman*, in violent heat and commotion; *dern*, hidden, secret.

REQUIEM

The swaws o the firth whammle and freeze til a wyce daith,
syne lown and douce tyne their micht in a flather o fraith,
but monie waters canna droun luve and faith.

Monie waters wi aa their sound, and the warld's stour,
ramstam rair o the cities, and siller's pityless pouer,
can clort, can brak, can whammle the body's bruckil fleur.

But the ruit bydes stieve i the yird, the luift carries the seed,
a braird o bairns renews the true and aefauld breed,
and memorie lives and grows when aa that can dee is deid.

swaws, waves; *firth*, estuary; *whammle*, overwhelm; *lown*, quiet; *douce*, gentle; *tyne*,
lose; *flather*, foamy, pouring; *fraith*, froth; *stour*, dust; *ramstam*, headlong; *siller*,
money; *clort*, filthy; *bruckil*, brittle; *stieve*, firm; *luift*, air; *braird*, crop, growth; *aefauld*,
simple, pure.

FERMER'S DEEIN

He turns awa frae life,
    frae the sun and the sterns,
wi hardly a word for his wife,
    or a curse for his bairns,
forfochten wi rowth o strife
    and man's puir concerns.

He's tyauvt wi kye and corn
    and scarce thocht why,
aamaist sin he was born.
    Nou Daith stilps by,
ohn hope, faith, fear, or scorn,
    fegs, he's blye.

sterns, stars; *forfochten*, worn out by fighting; *rowth*, abundance; *tyauvt*, worked hard,
been embarrassed; *stilps*, stalks with long strides; *ohn*, without; *blye*, cheerful, blithe.

66

SAINLESS

I hae stuid an hour o the lown midsimmer nicht
til twal o the knock i the leelang glamarie-licht
by the cherry-tree at the midden, luikan aa round.
There's never a steer owreby at the ferm-toun,
the reek gangs straucht i the luift, that's lither and gray,
wi an auntran gair o gowd i the North by the Tay.
The whyte muin owre Drumcarro, the Lomond shawan
purpie i the West, and a lane whaup caaan.

The ither birds are duin, but thon whaup's aye busy,
wi the dirlan bubble-note that maks ye dizzy,
the daft cratur's in luve, tho it's late i the year,
aa round Lucklaw he's fleean wi an unco steer.
There's a wheen stots owre i the park by the mansion-hous,
skemblan about whiles, dozent and douce,
and a rabbit nibbles amang our raspberry canes
for aa our wire and our traps and the lave o our pains.

But the feck o the hour I hae gowpit owre the dyke,
taen up wi a sicht thonder that I dinna like,
a day-auld cowt liggan doun i the gress
and the Clydesdale mear standan there motionless.
The hale hour she has made never a steer,
but stuid wi her heid forrit, rigid wi fear,
it's a wonder onie beast can haud sae still.
The fermer douts the cowt has the joint-ill,
that canna be sained. Ye'd speir gin his mither kens?
Ay, beasts hae their tragedies as sair as men's.

lown, quiet; *knock*, clock; *leelang*, livelong; *glamarie-licht*, glamour; *midden*, dungheap;
steer, stir, disturbance; *owreby*, over yonder; *ferm-toun*, farm-buildings; *reek*, smoke;
luift, sky; *lither*, softly undulating with clouds; *auntran*, occasional; *gair*, patch; *whaup*,
curlew; *dirlan*, vibrating; *unco*, unusual, excessive; *a wheen*, a few; *stots*, bullocks;
skemblan, shambling; *dozent*, sleepy; *douce*, sedate, gentle; *for aa*, in spite of all; *lave*,
rest; *feck*, most part; *gowpit*, gaped; *dyke*, wall; *taen up*, preoccupied; *cowt*, colt;
haud, hold; *douts*, suspects; *sained*, healed; *speir*, ask.

LUVE

Gie aa, and aa comes back
  wi mair nor aa.
Hain ocht, and ye'll hae nocht,
  aa flees awa.

AFTER LUNCH, EKALI
September 1st, 1939

Cicalas burst the air, a heat-haze quivers
  on the pale plain, the glittering olive-trees.
The aerodrome vibrates, Mount Parnes shivers,
  the tamarisks squirm like flames waved in a breeze.
In that fierce blaze the scorched rock-garden shimmers,
  even the white verandah dazzles our sight.
We step inside, where Dresden china glimmers
  and ivories gleam in this green-shaded light.

I became peeved outside. Too hot . . . As hot as
  Dante's Inferno. Now I can indulge
coolly in nick-nacks. Tanagra terra-cottas
  smile from their shelves, archaic vases bulge
seductively. My host displays his treasures,—
  rare coins, fine books, quaint bits of this and that.
We settle down and reminisce of pleasures
  had here and there . . . But Madame will not chat.

There is an awkward silence. Harsh and tireless
  choirs of cicalas make a shattering din.
Madame is restless, crosses to the wireless,
  twiddles the knobs, and gets, at last, Berlin.
Meine Entscheidung hab' ich jetzt getroffen
  die Polen auszurotten. Then *Sieg Heil! Sieg Heil!*
Did I hear right? Or am I *ganz besoffen*?
  This to the Reichstag . . . Well, it's done in style.

We do not speak, nor look at one another;
 between us now a deep cold gulph has sprung.
My hosts are German . . . It is hard to smother
 excited words that throng upon the tongue . . .
Now I am calm, and contemplate a glaucous
 columnar cypress by the garden fence.
I hardly hear the individual raucous
 shouts of the Fuehrer, but I know the sense.

My hostess says, *Gott sei Dank! Du bist Schotte.*
 Du bist kein Feind. Technically not so,
in view of 1707, I thought. But not a
 symptom of contradiction did I show.
Vous allez revenir après la guerre,
 they said, and beamed, but with a hopeless look.
En peu de temps, I answered, *je l'espère*,
 and wrote in Doric in their visitors' book:

Κόλπῳ ἐν ᾿Αδριακῷ καὶ ἐν αἱμασιαῖσιν ῾Εκάλας
 Σκωτὸς Γερμανοῖν συγγενόμαν φιλικῶς.
Νῦν δ᾿ ὁ χρόνος δεινός, καὶ ἐπὶ ξυροῦ ἵσταται ἀκμᾶς
 εἰράνα πόλεμός θ᾿ · ἁ δὲ μενεῖ φιλία.

THE TWENTY-THIRD PSALM O KING DAUVIT

Composed on St Andrew's Day, 1942, in Edinburgh Prison

The late Moray MacLaren in *The Scots* (1951) tells how "a Scottish writer who was speaking in support of a Scottish Nationalist political candidate at a rural district in the East Lowlands found himself at an informal meeting of farmers and small town business men. They asked him whether all this revival of the Scottish language was not 'so much nonsense,' and whether anything that he had written in this kind could really be understood by them— plain ordinary Scots folk. For an answer this rather peculiar-looking literary man, black-bearded and immensely elongated, drew himself up to his full six and a half feet and recited to them his own translation of the Twenty-third Psalm in Scots. When he had finished there was a long silence; and the present writer can vouch for it that one or two of these practical East Coast Lowland farmers were near to tears."

The Lord's my herd, I sall nocht want.
Whaur green the gresses grow
sall be my fauld. He caas me aye
whaur fresh sweet burnies rowe.

He gars my saul be blyth aince mair
that wandert was frae hame,
and leads me on the straucht smaa gait
for sake o His ain name.

Tho I suld gang the glen o mirk
I'ld grue for nae mischance,
Thou bydes wi me, Thy kent and cruik
maks aye my sustenance.

Thou spreids ane brod and gies me meat
whaur aa my faes may view,
Thou sains my heid wi ulyie owre
and pours my cogie fou.

Nou seil and kindliness sall gae
throu aa my days wi me,
and I sall wone in God's ain hous
at hame eternallie.

want, lack; *caas*, drives; *rowe*, roll; *gars*, makes; *straucht smaa gait*, straight narrow track; *mirk*, darkness; *grue*, feel a chill of horror; *bydes*, dost remain; *kent*, shepherd's long pole for leaping hedges, etc.; *cruik*, crook; *brod*, board, table; *meat*, food; *faes*, enemies; *sains*, dost bless; *ulyie*, oil; *cogie*, bowl; *seil*, blessing; *wone*, dwell.

70

THE SHEPHERD'S DOCHTER
Written on the occasion described in Fife in 1949

Lay her and lea her here i the gantan grund,
    the blythest, bonniest lass o the countryside,
    crined in a timber sark, hapt wi the pride
o hothous flouers, the dearest that could be fund.

Her faither and brithers stand, as suddentlie stunned
    wi the wecht o dule; douce neebours side by side
    wriest and fidge, sclent-luikan, sweirt tae bide
while the Minister's duin and his threep gane wi the wind.

The murners skail, thankfu tae lea thon place
    whar the blythest, bonniest lass liggs i the mouls,
    Lent lilies lowp and cypresses stand stieve,
Time tae gae back tae the darg, machines and tools
    and beasts and seeds, the things men uis tae live,
and lea the puir lass there in her state o Grace.

From *Chasing an Ancient Greek*

Hollis and Carter, London, 1950

An impressionistic autobiography, chiefly describing his European
travels to study the manuscripts of Theognis. The passage below
however deals with his views on Scottish conscription and the Act
of Union which led to his two terms of imprisonment. It arose out
of an explanation of his position which he gave to a private dinner
party including his German hosts and a Scots-American in Munich
in 1949.

BESIDES THIS MAIN AIM the S.N.P. was continually adopting resolutions
on all sorts of policies, and in 1937, after the failure of the League of
Nations had become manifest, its conference had considered the eventual-
ity of another world war and had resolved that members of military age
should not serve in the British Forces unless and until Scotland had her
own government. This was a pretty strong resolution, but no way out of
the ordinary for a national movement if one reflects on the history of
national movements in general. It struck me that, if one was to be serious
at all about self-government for Scotland, it was only proper to be most
serious about the most serious aspects of the question. Accordingly the
question of Scotland's position in a war was of more importance than the
incidence of infantile mortality, overcrowding in slums, electrification of
railways, construction of road-bridges over the Forth and Tay estuaries,
digging of a mid-Scotland ship-canal, and all the other stock-in-trade of
nationalist platforms.

It could be shown, indeed it was notorious, that in the 1914-18 war
Scotland had suffered disproportionately heavy casualties as compared
with any other part of the British Empire, through the English War Office's
reckless employment of Scots regiments in costly attacks; and Sir John
Boyd Orr and others had pointed out how much more Scotland's economy
had suffered than England's both from the war-time state-socialism based
on Whitehall and from the war's aftermath of slump and "rationalisation,"
which were much more severe in Scotland, having no government to look
after its interests, even than they were in England, whose governments,
though stupid, were at least primarily concerned with England. Therefore
it seemed to me obvious that there was no time when it was more important
for Scotland to have a say in her own affairs than in the upheavals of war.

How little small nations mattered to the rulers of England was only too clear when almost everybody in Parliament and out of it applauded Mr Neville Chamberlain's treatment of the Czechs as a remote small nation the British knew nothing about. Personally I happened to be quite keen on the Czechs, partly from my friendship with their great champions the Seton-Watsons, and also because Jan Masaryk, their Ambassador, had himself come and enlisted the sympathies of the Bryce Club at Oxford, a body of which I had been president, formed in memory of the Ulster Scot Lord Bryce, to promote understanding of international affairs. But logic compelled me to see that Scotland's claims on my services were far more urgent than those of the Czechs or the Poles, the English, Hottentots, or any other nation could be. This being so, I took the position that Scotland should have the same equality of rights within the British Commonwealth as Canada, New Zealand, and the other dominions, including the enlistment and control of her own forces for any alliance she might join.

When, after Hitler's seizure of Prague in spring, 1939, conscription was being debated in Britain, the question was raised in nationalist circles whether it was constitutionally valid in its application to Scotland, having regard to the terms of the Treaty of Union of 1707 which set up the United Kingdom of Great Britain and the British Parliament. The answer appeared to be that it was not constitutionally *intra vires* for the U.K. Parliament to conscribe the Scots for foreign service. At a May Day demonstration in Aberdeen a heckler asked me about the constitutional position arising out of the Treaty of Union, and I answered as above, with the concurrence of the crowd. Once I had expressed this opinion publicly, naturally I could not depart from it unless reasoned out of it; and in fact, the more the question was examined, the more clearly it seemed to me I was right; and it was from that conviction of mine that the litigation arose with the British Government three years later.

When Hitler invaded Poland I happened to be in Greece, and I did not reach Britain till nearly mid-September of 1939. Arriving in London in a black-out, and disliking the melancholy singing of hymns kept up pretty constantly by the staff in the hotel I had gone to, I took a run down to Oxford, where I found everyone sitting around as usual, sipping sherry and sofa-strategising with indefatigable ingenuity. Calling at the Clarendon buildings, where they were recruiting for various services, I asked if there was anything I could do, only to be told that as I was over 25 I was in a reserved occupation and could not do anything. This was the first I had heard, having been abroad, of the introduction of conscription. Its application to Scotland I had been resolved to oppose, and I was only confirmed in this by the information that the U.K. Parliament had not applied it to Northern Ireland, a gross discrimination against Scotland, especially in view of the fact that the Scots' treaty rights were being violated.

On going up to Scotland I found the phoney war in full swing, with a good deal of political confusion, extending to the nationalist movement, very few of the members of which saw clearly in any direction on any issue. Some were opposed to the war on pacifist grounds, or on socialist grounds, like Jimmie Maxton's Independent Labour Party; others were all for it, and wanted to volunteer for Finland when Russia commenced her campaign there; the general opinion was that, although in theory Scotland should have a say of her own, in practice there was little to do at that stage but conform to the British Government's requirements. I adhered to the position I had adopted in advance: Dominion self-government in war as in peace, and no acquiescence in the unconstitutional conscription, either for military purposes or, as was soon imposed, for industrial work.

The English bureaucracy had naturally seen to it that English industrialists got most of the contracts for war-work, and that most of the new factories were set up in England, while Scots works were turned over to storage and Scots workers conscribed away to places like Coventry and Wolverhampton. By the spring of 1942 public opinion in Scotland was restive about this: a debate in the Commons showed that most Scots M.P.s of all parties did not approve of it, any more than the trade unions, local authorities, and religious bodies which had been protesting against it. This was the background of public opinion when the British bureaucracy, having "dereserved" my age group, got around to prosecuting me in a sheriff-court for not complying with their call-up notice for medical examination for the Forces (for which in fact medical men had advised me I would not be fit, owing to certain defects of physique and health). There followed several interesting trials, punctuated by two terms in gaol and a Parliamentary by-election in which I was not far from being returned to Westminster. But the constitutional contentions I was making were never properly adjudicated. As the Scots-American was much interested in my account of them at the Munich dinner-party, perhaps others will be also.

The first Sheriff before whom I argued that the Treaty of Union conveyed no power to the U.K. Parliament to conscribe the Scots for foreign service was a worthy old fellow, who had been a keen soldier himself, and a Brigadier in the First World War. He listened respectfully to my contentions, which I delivered in a plain matter-of-fact way, congratulated me on my ability and learning, very much to the surprise and delight of the Press, and regretted that he must find me guilty and sentence me to twelve months' imprisonment, which was then the standard term for not complying with the military service acts. I appealed to the High Court of Justiciary, and was liberated on bail, when I proceeded to issue my defence as a pamphlet.

Some time before, I had been asked to be nominated as chairman of the council of the Scottish National Party, as it was felt that my friend Mr William Power, the veteran man of letters who was then chairman, was unable to deal with the position through age and the difficulties of war-time travel. While I was at large pending my appeal being heard the conference of the S.N.P. took place and by a small majority they elected me chairman, which led many people to recall the movement on Clydeside in the first war, when Tom Johnston's weekly *Forward*, which Bernard Shaw described as "the first paper worth a workman's tuppence," freely criticised the war and the Government, and was suppressed by Lloyd George for untimely candour. People rushed to the conclusion that I must be another turbulent tribune of the type of Davie Kirkwood or Willie Gallacher, and were surprised to find that in fact I discoursed about the current conflict with the same donnish sangfroid as I would lecture on the second Peloponnesian war or the siege of Saguntum.

Advocates and solicitors and others had meantime been giving me bits of advice on the arguing of my appeal in the High Court, and the result was a longish document, for which I take whatever blame or credit there may be, which Mr James Bridie the playwright was pleased to describe as "a noble piece of literature" but which passed over the heads of their Lordships like water off a duck's back. In the course of an hour and a half I argued four alternative contentions: That the National Service Act was

(1) contrary to the Common Law of Scotland, as was proved by references to a number of statutes and other constitutional actings;

(2) contrary to the Scotio-Anglic Treaty of Union which constituted the United Kingdom of Great Britain and the British Parliament;

(3) unknown to the Law of Scotland, being a statute of a foreign state, *viz.* the Kingdom of England;

(4) a fundamental nullity, being a pretended statute of what is now a legal non-entity, *viz.* the so-called Great Britain, which is deficient in the qualifications of a legal personality by International Law.

Some of my lawyer friends found some of these contentions more convincing than others, but they all looked forward to the judges expounding their answers to them. Instead of which the Court, in dismissing the appeal, made no reference to any contention I had made, and ascribed to me a fifth contention, which I had not made, namely: That all the acts of the imperial Parliament since 1707 were void and of no effect, a dummy proposition which they incontinently rejected. Their handling of the case did not add to their lustre in their own profession, to judge from the views bandied about by other judges and by advocates, and expressed to me and others privately with the canniness one would expect from the Scots legal fraternity. Nor did they allow the case to be published in the usual way in the law reports, in spite, or because, of the interest it had aroused.

Consequently I was conveyed away in a Black Maria to the prison at Saughton, on the outskirts of Edinburgh, and kept there for eight months, securing the normal remission for prisoners who do not break the regulations. My health suffered a bit, but it was by no means boring, all the less so as the Secretary of State for Scotland, Tom Johnston, who had in 1927 moved a Bill in Parliament to withdraw the Scots M.P.s from Westminster and set up a Scottish Parliament with the powers of the Dominion of Canada, took advantage of the prison regulations facilitating the educational uplift of the inmates to enable me to carry on a commentary I was doing on Theognis, so that I had Homer, Aeschylus, Sophocles, Pindar, and a great many more companions in my cell. The disadvantage of reading Homer in gaol, I may mention, is that the noble carnivorous repasts of the heroes tend to rouse appetites which the prison diet cannot appease. On weekdays I used to work about the grounds in what was called "the garden party," and on Sundays play a wheezy old harmonium for the Presbyterian services in the chapel, the voluntary most in request being Handel's *Largo*. It added to the gaiety of the nation when Dr Robert McIntyre, secretary of the National Party, organised a procession complete with bagpipes to serenade me at the prison-gates, the poet Hugh MacDiarmid being among the most demonstrative of the demonstrators.

In odd moments I also wrote a good deal of verse, some of it quite good, including a long series of Limericks on the Governor, Chaplain, warders, and inmates, which gained a considerable, if restricted, currency, and gave rise to a vast range of popular variants, mostly in the direction of hair-raising obscenity, which eventually found their way to me, often on pieces of paper designed by the manufacturer for humbler purposes than writing. Russian books too were allowed me in the way of uplift: I worked through Anna Semeonoff's exercises very conscientiously, and read a good deal of Maurice Baring's anthology, translating some pieces, but have never had time to keep it up since liberation, much as I like the tongue. There was an intelligent old lag who had learned German from a Pole on a previous stretch and had become curious about Immanuel Kant, so I got the *Kritik der reinen Vernunft* sent in, and discussed some points in it with him, in German; yet his common form of crime was the most reckless house-breaking; for example, heaving a brick through a furrier's window to hand out a mink coat to a noctambule lady friend, he had been so short-sighted as to hand one to a policeman.

My old father came in one day to visit me. He was a Tory, and a British Imperialist, having been an officer in the Bengal Artillery; but quite a steady nationalist on many non-political issues. For instance, he was always annoyed to hear of any of his female relatives marrying a Sassenach, almost as if they had espoused a coloured person. At first he did not at all approve my political nationalism, especially when it went the length of not joining the Army and even of landing in gaol. But he was becoming reconciled to the situation by the time of his visit: when he went as an elder to the Presbytery of Cupar some of the Ministers and elders had congratulated him on my stand for Scottish rights, and he had happened to learn, at a family funeral, of some distant ancestral connection with one of the Scots Jacobites who had been hanged, drawn, and quartered by the English after the failure of the 1745 Rising, Sir John Wedderburn of Blackness, so that he jocularly told the warder in charge of the interview that I was not the first political prisoner in the family.

The students of Edinburgh University had the bright idea of nominating me as their Lord Rector, and carried out a campaign against the shift south of Scots workers, especially of young women and girls, which Ernest Bevin was then carrying out, in spite of Scots protests. They plastered the quadrangle with provocative slogans, such as "If Young is wrong, Laval is right," and freely denounced as quislings all those who defended Scotland's subordination to England under the present union: the majority of the students, however, very sensibly preferred to re-elect their previous Rector, an opulent local philanthropist.

Not long after my emergence from this first prison-term, having reached the Platonic age of thirty I duly got married to my predestined part-Basque; but the honeymoon in the Highlands was hardly over when a parliamentary seat fell vacant in Kirkcaldy Burghs, in my native county of Fife, and I was asked to contest the by-election. This I did with some diligence, haranguing miners at the pithead, shipbuilders and linoleum-workers in their lunch-hour, or canvassing housewives in shopping queues and young couples waiting for the next house at the cinema. I promised, if elected, to seek to promote a Bill to give Scotland Dominion status, like the British North America Act of 1867 which set up the Dominion of Canada.

The main emphasis of the campaign was on the illegality and undesirability of military and industrial conscription of the Scots by any other government than one directly responsible to the Scottish people themselves. It was remarkable how many telegrams and letters of support came from officers and men of the 51st Highland Division in Italy and other Scots units, and from working people who had been dragooned away to work in England. The other candidates were a local Labour town councillor, who supported Mr Churchill's coalition government, and a pacifist, who stood under the title of "Christian Socialist." When they counted the votes the Coalition man had 52 per cent and I had 42 per cent, on which the leading Conservative newspaper in Scotland (*The Scotsman*) commented:

> There is here something which the Government and the Scottish Office must take note of. Mr Douglas Young is a fervid Scottish Nationalist who refused from conviction to obey the law of a Government whose authority to conscribe Scotsmen he denied. Kirkcaldy Burgh electors, instead of ridiculing his constitutional claim, went to the polls and voted for him in very large numbers.

The Government no doubt took note. In fact, I was told, the matter came to the Cabinet, where Mr Ernest Bevin insisted on commencing a new prosecution against me, this time on the matter of industrial, not of military, conscription, which duly developed later in that year. Meantime, in spring 1944, I had drafted a statement of Scotland's claim for Dominion status, which the National Party council submitted to the Dominion Prime Ministers. They all replied stating they were in favour of it, except Mr Curtin, who declined to commit himself. There were two Scotsmen among the favourable Premiers, the Liberal Mackenzie King, of Canada, and the Gaelic-speaking Socialist Peter Fraser, of South Africa [*sic*]. Sir Godfrey Huggins, of Southern Rhodesia, an Englishman, also came out firmly in favour, as did Field-Marshal Smuts, of South Africa, one of the most respected statesmen of the Commonwealth. When I mentioned this to my friends at Munich the Scots-American interrupted: "Gee, why didn't you approach that old snake Roosevelt?" Answer: because he owed no allegiance to the British Crown. "Maybe not, but I guess the old British Crown owed plenty to him."

The Ministry of Labour having proceeded against me for refusing to come and see a bureaucrat about a job, I was haled into another Sheriff-Court, presided over by a rather deaf and testy old gentleman, who kept interrupting and seemed not to understand what was said to him, nor to have very clear views what the case was about. Convicting as a matter of routine, he imposed the routine maximum sentence of three months' imprisonment. It was curious that even those who had approved the first sentence imposed on me, two years before, exclaimed against this second one, and the hearing of the appeal I lodged was awaited with considerable interest (October, 1944).

My contentions on this occasion were two: (1) that authorisation of the regulation I was charged with contravening was beyond the powers conveyed to the U.K. Parliament by the Treaty of Union; (2) alternatively, that even if that were not so, the Minister of Labour and his officers had no authority to ignore Article XVIII of the Treaty of Union in giving effect to the regulation. It will be noted that neither of these contentions is the same as any of the four alternative contentions I had made in 1942, and that the Act under which I was now prosecuted was not the same act as had been adduced on the previous occasion: nor was the alleged offence the same. Nevertheless the Court, consisting of a different set of judges this time, appeared to have formed in advance the conclusion that I was about to submit the same proposition as the previous set of judges had, quite wrongly, ascribed to me and rejected. Therefore they incontinently refused to hear the appeal, and committed me to gaol.

On legal advice I then sought to take advantage of an old right of the Scots, protestation for remeid of law, which had been employed on some famous occasions, for example by Andrew Fletcher of Saltoun, the chief opponent of the Treaty of 1707, and which was part of the sphere of Scots Law reserved from alteration by the United Kingdom Parliament under that Treaty. Members of Parliament made efforts to take up my case in the Commons, but were met with refusals and even lies by the Government spokesmen.

In sum, the issues were never adjudicated, and it was by no means apparent that justice had been done in either case. If there was a denial of justice, it was the more grave in that it involved the right of personal liberty, the most valuable right of the subjects in Scotland, under the Treaty of Union with England, the very origin and legal basis of the United Kingdom of Great Britain and the British Parliament. The question raised was, of course, that of federal constitutionalism, a question perfectly familiar to every American and Australian, as the Scots-American at this Munich dinner-party immediately saw. It was not enough for a sheriff or other judge to take refuge behind an Act of the Westminster Parliament if that Parliament itself had its powers restricted by an Act of two Parliaments, namely the terms of union, an international treaty, between Scotland and England. The English have been accustoming themselves to the dogma of the omnipotence of Parliament, but such a dogma is untenable in relation to Scotland, whose Parliament was never omnipotent, and is incompatible with the Treaty of Union which constituted the British Parliament to begin with.

The relevance of the question to contemporary Europe is only too apparent, when one considers the movement for a federal union of the western states, the conferences at the Hague, Strasbourg, and so on. The insular English, with their peculiar dogma that one is better without any rational constitution and that a legislature should be allowed to please itself and govern at discretion, naturally find a difficulty in seeing eye to eye with Continentals as soon as they begin to come down to brass tacks about constituting the desired union. It was quite interesting that at Strasbourg the British representative who most commended himself to Continental opinion was an Australian Scot, R. W. G. Mackay, who has publicly declared his support for the establishment of a Scots and a Welsh Parliament and the federalisation of the nations of the British Isles as a contribution to the extension of federalisation in Europe. Things are never settled finally till they are settled justly, and there will be no just or satisfactory international order in Europe till each nation of Europe has its due, equality of rights in its own affairs, with all contributing a due share to the common obligations of the whole group, however wide it be. On this view my litigation about the Treaty of Union may be seen as a slight contribution to a rationally united Europe, and my only regret is that the lawyers and statesmen are so hesitant in taking the matter further.

The Scots-American cottoned on to the idea all right, and grew quite enthusiastic about Scotland having her own place in the world, going over all the Scots diplomats he had known who could represent us, and generally exploring all the implications. The Rhinelander urbanely expressed surprise at my legalistic fervour, and our hostess thought it was getting cold on the balcony, so we went in, and the American drove me to my hotel, bubbling over with patriotic enthusiasm, warmer than my own, because more novel. There is a Scots diaspora of twenty million like him.

Dialect and Standard English

A letter to *The Scotsman* of 24 October 1952 in a controversy with
an Orkney schoolmaster who was strongly in favour of suppressing
local dialects.

Makarsbield, Tayport, Fife
October 16, 1952

SIR,—Mr Thorburn places us in his debt by expounding the viewpoint
of an Orkney head master in relation to the Advisory Council's reports on
Scottish education. It might be helpful at this stage to consider the general
recommendation, para. 623 of the 1947 Report (Cmd. 7005), on the Train-
ing and Attitude of (rural) Teachers, where I read:

"It is for them to convey to their pupils that 'the country' means far
more than a place of abode or livelihood, is indeed a distinctive way of
life, which, even if it lacks certain urban amenities and rewards, retains
its immemorial power to satisfy many of the deepest and noblest instincts
of our human nature."

Surely the homely local speech is a vital element in this "distinctive
way of life," and if official policy seeks to stifle it in favour of a standard
urban dialect (be it of Queen's English or Court Scots), then Authority is
tearing up by the roots one of the soundest and most necessary elements
in the community.

Standard English is, of course, now a world-auxiliary language, and
Orkney bairns should learn to read, write, and speak it, just as Scandina-
vian or Soviet children learn it, for the access it gives to fields of science,
history, philosophy, literature, commerce, and affairs, that are not within
the range of spoken Orkney Norn or of Braid Scots, however spoken or
written, or of any merely national language, like Italian, Swedish,
Georgian. As part of their European cultural heritage one would like to
see them get Latin also (which Stalin is ordering to be taught in 32,000
schools of the U.S.S.R., and which was the language of educated Scotland
in the days of the Arbroath Declaration and for more centuries than any
kind of English has been): also Greek and French: and, as an integral part
of the Scottish heritage, Gaelic.

But an educational system can impart the great languages of international culture, or some of them, without simultaneously wiping out the
traditional dialect of a local community, which is so important to its
stability and cohesion. Italy, Switzerland, Belgium afford readily accessible

examples, which our insular educational authorities, with their London-dominated notions, seem not to have noted.

I agree with the Advisory Council's deprecation (Primary report, par. 307) of certain debased *patois* of Scots, and in particular our teachers might check the spread of the glottal stop, which will make our tongue as cacophonous as Danish if we let it; but I do not class the Orkney speech, as I heard it in Birsay, Stronsay, or Kirkwall, with the Hibernicised slang of the Cowcaddens or the pouter-pigeon English of Kelvinside, which are spurious distortions lacking the genuine authochthonous savour. The Advisory Council tilt at a windmill when they say, "We cannot recapture the fine 'Scottis' of the courts of James IV and V," as if one should dismiss the proposal to inculcate standard English as a utopian scheme to recapture the King's Wessex of Alfred the Great or the quaint twang of the Tudor Elizabeth, with samples of which the Third Programme bumbazed many genteel lugs.

The Scottish Home Service has, in fact, been spreading for 20 years a semi-standard cultivated Scots, derived from what R. L. Stevenson termed "Sir Walter's brave metropolitan utterance." The same "homely, natural, and pithy everyday speech" which the Advisory Council states "is not the language of 'educated' people anywhere, and could not be described as a suitable medium of education or culture," is, in fact, at the command of some well-known Edinburgh platform personalities, such as Sir Alexander Gray, chairman of the B.B.C.'s panel on broadcasting for Scottish schools; Mr Albert Mackie, and Mr Robert Kemp; and is capable of development into a medium of culture as its ancestor was a few generations ago, at least to the degree at which Flemish and Afrikaans are to-day employed in universities and public life.

Pending such a development, while teachers may not actively encourage Scots, they do ill to discourage it, especially in view of the explicit recommendation (par. 309 of the Primary report) that "a short but definite weekly period should be set aside exclusively for Scottish traditions and language," and the Council's desire "to give this study a dignity of its own."

Mr Thorburn fears that his pupils will be at a disadvantage in seeking posts of high emolument if they cannot speak a fluent standard English. Time was when a guid Scots tongue in an applicant's head was thought by employers to portend certain qualities of intellect and character; but it may be nowadays that certain "urban amenities and rewards" are open to the lad o' pairts from South Ronaldshay only if he contrives to sound as if he came from South Kensington.

If it is public policy to deracinate our food-producers to swell the megalopolitan mass of glib bureaucrats and slick stenographers, let Mr Shearer's standard of linguistic values be endorsed. If not, not.—I am &c.

DOUGLAS YOUNG.

On Being an Estuary Bird

From the *Glasgow Herald* of 4 July 1953 in praise of the Tay.

WHY, PEOPLE ASK ME, why have you stuck yourself in Tayport, an obscure hole in an out-of-the-way corner of Fife? Because, I tell them, Tayport is the pleasantest place to live in that I have found in Europe.

From Athens in the South to Stockholm in the North, I have gone questing; and from Dublin in the West to Moscow in the East. But for a place to live in I have never yet found any to equal Tayport.

The most important aspects of a place for living were set out long ago by the founder of scientific medicine, the Greek Hippocrates, whose oath our medical men yet swear. He wrote a treatise "On Airs, Waters, and Places," in which he stressed the importance of site and climate and of the local presence of waters. In all these I find that Tayport is most pleasant, most temperate, best balanced. And all this follows from its being, not only on an estuary, but on the best of all estuaries, and at the best point of the estuary.

A little reflection shows that estuaries form the environment most suited to the human personality on earth, with the finest intermixture of variety and stability in the surrounding scene that confronts the eye, the master-organ of sense.

The worst sites are in marshes—Minsk, for example, the capital of Byelo-Russia, is never likely to contribute largely to the elevation of human culture. Only less bad are the great plains and plateaux, as at Milan. A sizeable river flowing through a town is, to be sure, a redeeming feature, even on a flattish landscape like the Danube at Budapest or the Neva at Leningrad. And there is much merit in lakes, as at Geneva and Zurich. Even a valley is an advantage, as for Innsbruck between its mountain walls, or Heidelberg in its wooded hills.

But rivers and valleys imply a one-way movement, a monotonous rhythm in a single direction, whereas a tidal estuary implies the majestic recurrence of complementary impulses, an enantiodromic stability deeply symbolic for human life. A mere tide, as on any sea coast, is hardly enough, for it may be barely perceptible, as at Copenhagen by the Baltic or at Venice on its brackish lagoons. Estuaries give you most markedly the feeling of being poised between two elements and two movements, the sense of the interaction of sea and land, of life and death and rebirth.

Life came, on this earth, from the sea. Our globe's surface began as a sea of fire, and will end as a sea of ice. It is by estuaries that we live closest to the eternal verities, the ebb and flow of mortal things, the Heraclitean flux, what Chinese philosophers call *yin* and *yang*.

Coventry Patmore put the tidal rhythm tellingly into some verses:

> Here, in this little bay,
> Full of tumultuous life and great repose,
> Where twice a day
> The purposeless glad ocean comes and goes. . . .

He concludes by expressing the feeling of estuary-dwellers that we may have confidence in the ultimate rightness of the sum of things:

> For want of me the world's course will not fail.
> When all its work is done the lie shall rot.
> Great is the Truth, and shall prevail
> When none cares whether it prevail or not.

Those who live by the outflow of great tidal rivers attain thereby a sense of balance and tranquillity.

It was by rivers that the oldest civilisations arose; higher forms of civilisation sprang up by seas; and the more tidal the seas the higher the development of the civilisation. Tidal firths indeed afford the perfect site for civilised living. The geopoliticians appear so far to have overlooked the probability that it was precisely because Scotland is so rich in estuaries that our discriminating ancestors chose it to settle in. As was remarked in the Arbroath Declaration of 1320, the Scots originated somewhere near the Caucasus, at the eastern extremity of Europe, and traversed thousands of miles, examining different territories, before wisely resolving to colonise Scotland.

Now we have many and notable estuaries, from the Solway and the Clyde, round by the white sands of Morar to Ythan, as far south as the Tweed. But, after personally inspecting most of them, I am convinced that eastward-opening firths have a general superiority to those that flow west, north, or south. For the flow against the sun's course better maintains that sense of enantiodromic equilibrium, of constant variation within a stable frame of reference, that makes the special emotional quality of estuary-dwelling.

The Tay, moreover, is our greatest river, drawing down from among the little red saxifrages on the snow-fed screes of Ben Lui, swelled by a myriad burns, flowing by historic places, to culminate at Tayport and join that world-encircling highway of brine, the open sea.

Mere eastward expansion is not enough: the actual size and proportions of a firth are very important also. And in these aspects the Tay estuary is perfect, as viewed from Tayport, and above all from my own study window. On Solway the disproportion is too great between the firth at ebb and the flooded estuary; on Forth it is too small; at Morar the river meandering through the white sands is a mere trickle at low tide compared to the full basin, and the same objection may be urged against the Esk at Montrose; the surrounding landscape of the Ythan is too paltry.

But here, at Tayport, it is just a mile of glittering strait from our harbour mouth to the old castle of Broughty on its Angus promontory; and then, eastward, the firth expands to some three miles in glorious sweeping bays of golden sand and green links, when the tide floods up and the basin brims full, shining in the sun, gleaming in the moonlight, a myriad different shades as the seasons and days shift and the clouds wander over.

And when it ebbs, twice in a day and night, Tay does not dwindle too far, but remains a majestic stream a mile and a half wide, between expanses of richly hued alluvial soils, patterned with endlessly varying pools and streamlets. On one side lie the wooded hills of Angus, backed by the splendid curves of the Sidlaws, and the purple ranges beyond of the Mownth, which tourists call the Grampians from a misprint in Tacitus. And here on our Fife side are moors and forests reaching to the Eden, and the last spurs of the Ochils running down among woods and farmlands to the rocks and sands.

No landscape, no seascape can compete with firthscape, the inter-animation of both elements, ever changing and conflicting, but always with the fundamental reconciliation that brings a saining to the soul.

A Note on Scottish Gaelic Poetry

An appendix to *Scottish Poetry*, a volume of essays from various
contributors, edited by James Kinsley, Cassel, London, 1955.

No BETTER POETRY has been written in Scotland in the last fifteen years
than the Gaelic poems by Somhairle MacGhillEathain (Sorley Maclean)
and George Campbell Hay. And in the last fifteen centuries perhaps the
best poetry produced in Scotland has been, on the whole, that in Gaelic.
There has been no Gaelic Burns, no Gaelic Dunbar, no Gaelic Hugh
MacDiarmid; but the language itself has long been cultivated for poetry,
and there is possibly a greater volume of excellently felt utterance in
Gaelic, by over a hundred poets, than has been achieved by all the Lallan
makars since John Barbour, all the Scots Latinists since Buchanan, and
all the Scots versifiers in English since Drummond of Hawthornden.

Naturally those brought up speaking Gaelic, and schooled in its
literature and in those of more fashionable tongues, are better able to
judge of this than one who, like the present writer, has no colloquial
fluency or literary command of the language. But we are not deterred from
criticizing Homer, Pindar and Theocritus through inability to speak their
dialects; if one can wield a dictionary and a grammar-book, and if one
undertakes the not excessive and highly intriguing study of the pronunciation of written Gaelic, there is a rich store of exciting verse in print, much
of it now with English versions *en face* to aid the reader. Without probing
very deeply into all the nuances of vocabulary and allusion, or mastering
the intricacies of accidence, even a superficial reader will be rewarded by
the musical range of the versification and by the frequent power and
brilliance of the imagery and declamation.

Gaelic-speaking society in Scotland has been for most of its course
fairly near to the spirit of Pindar's culture, a people of peasants, artisans
and seafarers, with a keen sense alike of heroism and of fun, and a brisk
ear for effect in assonance and rhythm of language and in the striking
juxtaposition of observation and reflection. Taking Celtic, and especially
Scots Gaelic, literature in its whole extent, there is no justification for the
notion that the poets were mainly preoccupied with twilight and moon-
shine, decay and death. It is as vivid and realist and varied a body of
literature as has been produced by any of the great languages and language-
groups at comparable stages of social development, as may be seen from

Professor Kenneth Jackson's anthology of translations into English, by himself, *A Celtic Miscellany* (1951). What is lacking to Gaelic verse is, in general, that which is lacking to Homer or Pindar—a modern sophistication abreast of the atomic cosmopolitan age. Yet even here Sorley Maclean's *An Cuilithionn* (1939: not yet printed in full) shows the entire capacity of the spoken and traditional language to deal with *avant-garde* themes at least as expressively as anyone has dealt with them in any other tongue.

It is perhaps permissible for me to explain, on a personal note, that at this writing I am in no way filled with the *furor Celticus* which is frequently to be observed taking hold of some Scot or other on first discovering in a receptive frame of mind the distinctive values of our Gaelic heritage, scenic, sartorial, bibulous, musical, linguistic, saltatory and the rest. I have been more or less continually exposed to most of them for a quarter of a century and more; have wielded an eager lexicon on a great deal of verse and substantial tracts of prose; and have even turned some thousands of lines of Gaelic poetry into English or Scots metre or rhythm. But my main interests have long lain in other tongues, chiefly Greek and Latin, and I now pen these notes calmly and without enthusiasm, to give a half-outsider's impression of what the inquiring poetry-lover may hope to find on looking into Scottish Gaelic.

First and chiefly, a rich language for poetic expression, much richer in mere sounds than English, French or German, for example; as rich, deep and wide in vocal tone as Russian or Italian. Word-music is much more prominent among the aims of Gaelic poets, as of Welsh, than it has been in the dominant literatures of classical or modern Europe. But there has long been also an astonishingly copious vocabulary, with whose range and subtleties no lexicon has yet contrived to cope with anything like adequacy. I first began to realize the fact when trying to pick English adjectives for the range of Gaelic terms expressive of beauty that Sorley Maclean employs in his *Dàin do Eimhir* (1943). A long tract of time, and the efforts of generations of poets and patrons and critical audiences, must be assumed at the back of this result. Fifteen centuries of ancestral Gaelic poetry is certainly no understatement of the period involved. Though James Macpherson, who in 1760 aroused Europe by his English version of Ossianic lays, is now understood to have had somewhat the same relation to his original sources as Sir Walter Scott had in editing Border ballads, it is certain that till the eighteenth century and later in Scotland and her western isles there were current scores of thousands of lines of

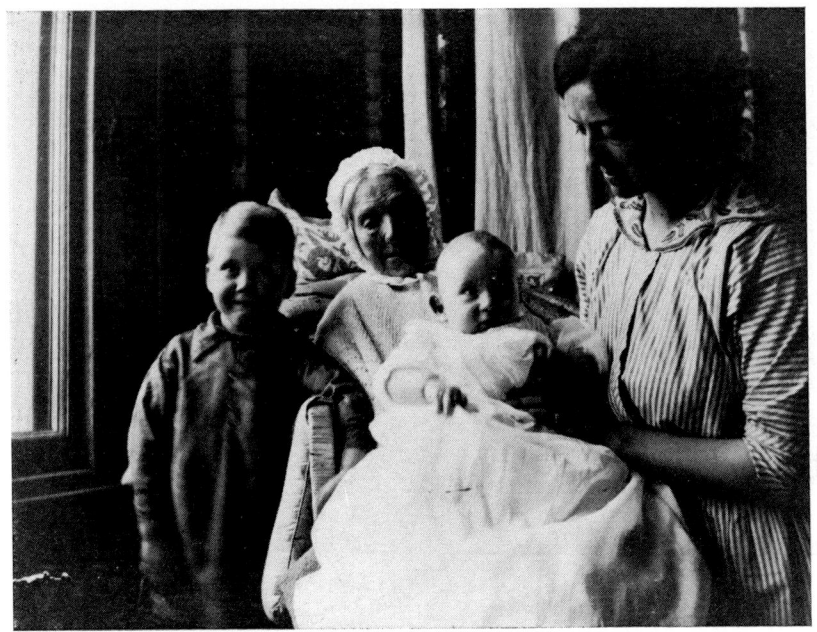

At Tayport in 1913 with his mother, Margaret Young, his great grandmother, "Grannie Greig," and his brother, John

Stephen Young in later life

Wearing his sailor's suit

At Merchiston Prep., 1925. Douglas is wearing spectacles. On his left is
Ian Robertson, the present Lord Robertson

In his study at Oxford, 1935. His specially made chair is five foot high

Laying a wreath at Wallace's statue, Aberdeen Wallace Commemoration, 1947

Above
Haranguing the public at Kirkcaldy

Top Right
The Copenhagen P.E.N. Congress, 1948. With (*left to right*) Richard Hughes, Peter Freuchen and Naomi Mitchison

Bottom Right
Tolstoy's diningroom at Yasnaya Polyana with portrait of Tolstoy by Repin. A party of six British writers—supporters of the Authors' World Peace Appeal—were invited to visit Russia by the Union of Soviet Writers in 1952. *Left to right:* A. E. Coppard, Richard Mason, D.Y., Naomi Mitchison, Doris Lessing and Arnold Kettle

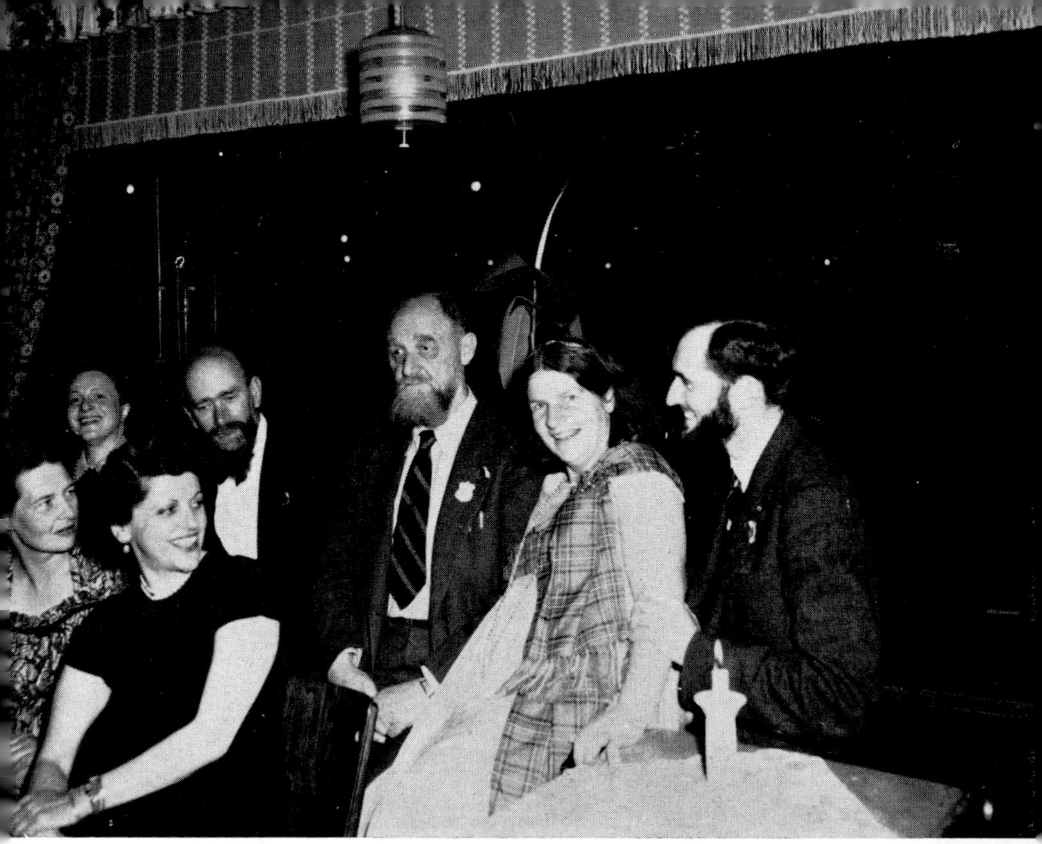

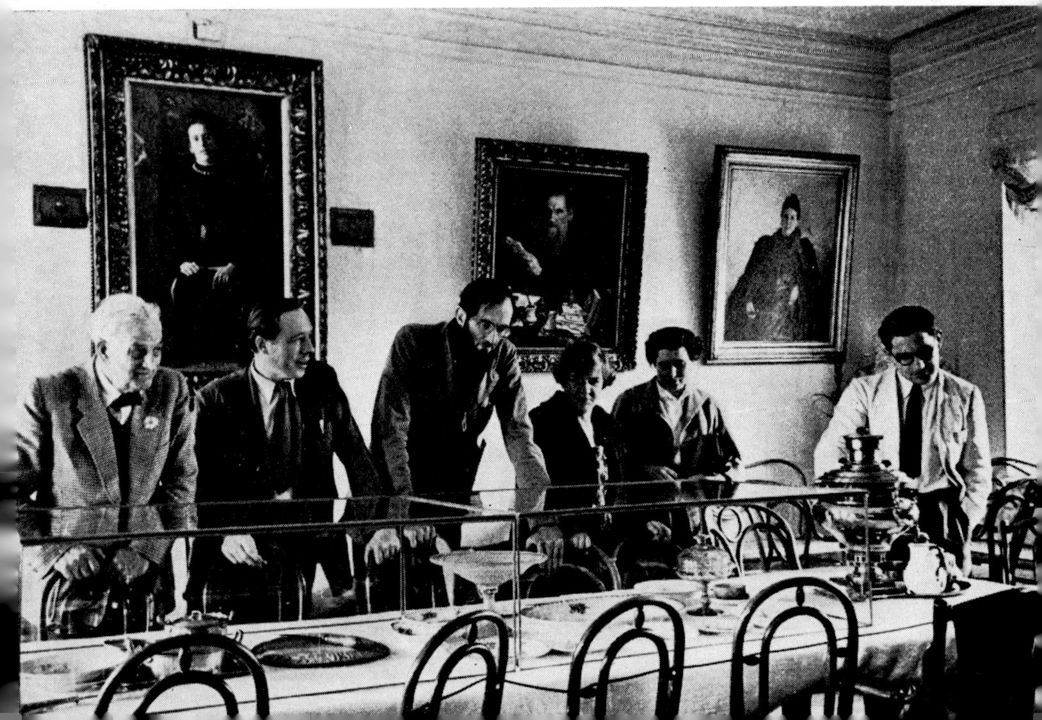

Above

With Hella and daughters Clara and Yana in the summerhouse at Makarsbield, 1954. Photograph taken by a *Picture Post* photographer

Top Right

With Compton MacKenzie and R. E. Muirhead at R. B. Cunninghame Graham centenary, Glasgow 1952

Bottom Right

With Tom Fleming and Abd'Elkader Farrah, the producer and designer of *The Burdies*, Edinburgh Festival, 1966

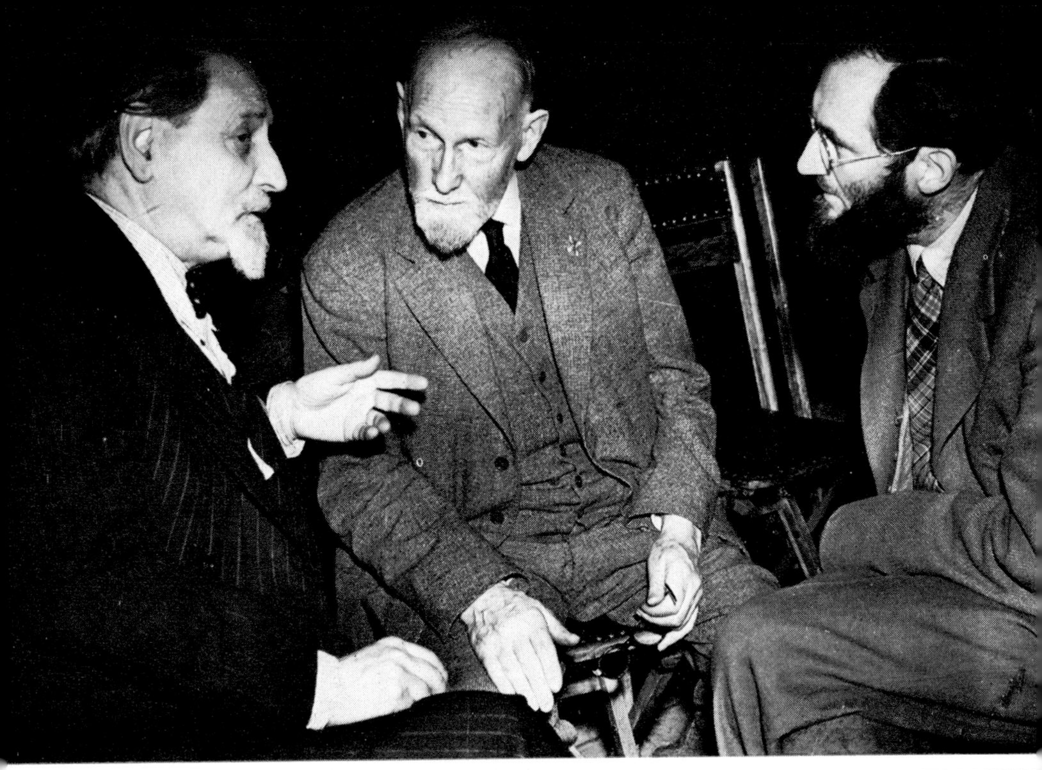

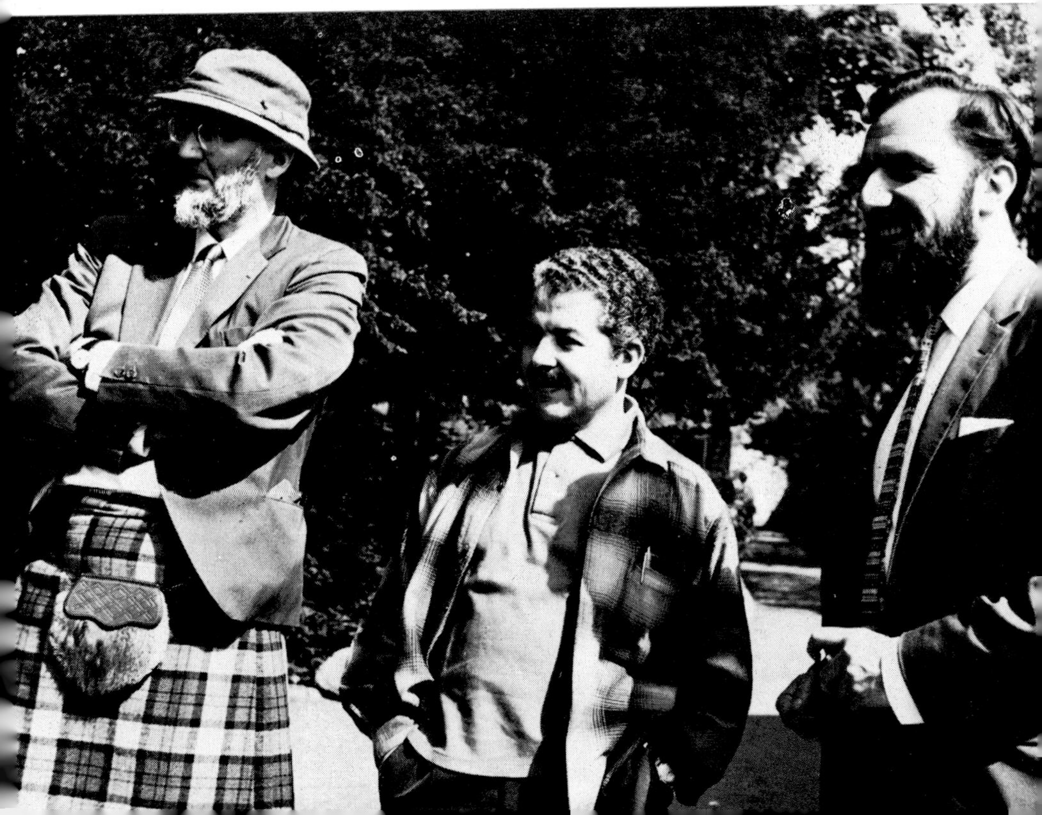

At Delos, Greece, April 1963

heroic saga verse. J. F. Campbell of Islay, in his *Leabhar na Féinne* (1872), printed some 54,000 lines of it independently of "Ossian" Macpherson's works; and much other material is extant in mediaeval manuscripts or other manuscripts earlier than Macpherson. This "Ossianic" epic cycle has Irish offshoots, but its bulk is centred in Scotland north of the Antonine Wall from Forth to Clyde. Though the invaders who are repelled are the Norsemen and Danes, the ethic is pre-Christian, on a Homeric level indeed, and the time when the poetic conglomeration crystallized cannot be placed long after the Roman Empire abandoned southern Britain in the fifth century.

Just as Homeric diction influenced all later Greek verse and prose, so what may be loosely termed "Ossianic" or heroic vocabulary and aesthetic effects pervaded Gaelic work till the most recent times. The society was aristocratic, but not so strongly divided horizontally as more opulent and settled aristocracies, because the vertical divisions of locality and clanship counted for a great deal in the struggle for existence. It was also cosmopolitan, relatively to the possibilities of the Middle Ages, with clerics and mercenaries and merchants travelling far afield and bringing home ideas and skills; it had its own physicians, astrologers, theologians and the like, as well as lawyers and soldiers. Till the Reformation in the sixteenth and seventeenth centuries Ireland and Scotland were more or less a single cultural area. Irish chiefs offered the crown of Ireland to James V, father of Mary Queen of Scots, when Henry VIII of England broke with Rome; just as Robert Bruce's brother Edward had for a time been King of Ireland, while the Scots had a naval base in the Isle of Man. The Celtic continuum from Scotland into Wales had been broken earlier, by the penetration of the Angles to the west coast of Cumberland; but as late as the Wars of the Roses we find Scots nobles banding with Welshmen and Marcher Lords in temporary coalitions, and no doubt tunes and musical idioms made their way from country to country, even after the Celtic tongues were dissimilated to the point of mutual unintelligibility.

Long poems were declaimed or chanted to the harp, a small portable *clàrsach* akin to the Welsh *crwth*. Lyrics were commonly made to a specified tune; and satires would tend to adopt the established line and stanza forms of epic or lyric. Drama did not develop, though there are elements of drama, and of the novel, in the poetic prose tales and in longer verse ballads. In the fifteenth-century "Flyting" of the courtly Dunbar with the aristocratic Kennedy, who was sib to the King, it is overt that Kennedy was a Gaelophile, and not hard to discern that Dunbar's richness of assonance and fancy owes much to a pervasive Celtic ambience in which he moved.

The first individual figure discernible in this ambience lived at the start of the thirteenth century, one Muireadhach Albannach ("Murdoch of Scotland," presumably to distinguish him from an Irish namesake). He is eponymous forebear of the MacVurichs, hereditary bards to the Macdonalds of Clanranald, and *sennachies* as well, charged to recite their history. In 1411, when Donald Balloch, Lord of the Isles, asserted his claim to the feudal Earldom of Ross by bringing some ten thousand clansmen to a sanguinary conflict at Harlaw, near Aberdeen, against the Regent Albany's forces commanded by Alexander Stewart, Earl of Mar, Big Lachlan MacVurich delivered a metrical "pep-talk" to the West Highlanders, consisting of 338 lines, divided into sections by letters of the Gaelic alphabet, and containing over 600 epithets appropriate to martial ardour. One would expect an absurd concoction of the type of:

> Austrian armies, awfully arrayed,
> Boldly with batteries besieged Belgrade:
> Cossack commanders cannonading come . . .

But MacVurich's incitement does achieve an effect that Pindar or Tyrtaeus might have envied.

Later in the fifteenth century we find a lady who has been compared to Sappho for the delicate and controlled passion with which she declares in verse a love that cannot be consummated: Isabel Stewart, heiress of Lorne (*d.* 1510), married by 1465 to Colin, second Lord Campbell, first Earl of Argyll, ambassador to England and France, Master of the Royal Household and Lord Chancellor, one of the richest and most cosmopolitan of the Scottish nobility. A contemporary, Effric MacCorquodale, widow of Hector MacTorquil MacNeill, constable of Castle Sween, commands effective metre and diction to deplore the acquisition of that stronghold by the Campbells. Lady Argyll's nephew, Sir Duncan Campbell of Glenorchy and Lawers, killed at Flodden in 1513, showed a strong vein of satire and popular humour. From the Flodden time we have a manuscript anthology, *The Book of the Dean of Lismore*, compiled about 1512-20 by a cleric from Perthshire, Sir James MacGregor, where the heroic and the recent are juxtaposed.

For learned bard and aristocratic patron and dilettante the classic metre was syllabic, metrical units of a determinate number of syllables being built up into hundreds of different stanza-types. Rhyme, assonance and alliteration were ornaments, sometimes elaborate. But in the sixteenth century, alike in Ireland and Scotland, the tendency developed to abandon regularity of syllable-grouping for rhythms based on a fixed number of stressed syllables, unstressed ones being allowed licences, by a process akin to Gerard Manley Hopkins's "sprung rhythm." The burden of erudition was diminished, and poets from humbler ranks of society produced more "folksy" utterances than had been usual—unless we are misled by the chances of preservation through anthologists' personal tastes and other causes.

Mary Macleod, Màiri nighean Alasdair Ruaidh (*c.* 1615-1707), may be reckoned the Corinna of Skye, making great verse unto her own clan, chiefly in elegies or panegyrics, which reveal the dominant values of the society in fitting tones. During her long life flourished also Iain Lom, John Macdonald, of the Keppoch family (*c.* 1620-*c.* 1710), who has stirring pieces on the battle of Inverlochy, the execution of Montrose, and other noteworthy episodes of the time. Though these are eminent single figures to whom a good volume of work attaches, much of the finest poetry appears in scattered items whose authors are either now anonymous or known by little else. For example, we have *Griogal Cridhe*, a passionately direct utterance, stark, simple and deeply moving when sung to the right tune—a lullaby to her child by the widow of a Gregor MacGregor, beheaded by her own brother, a Campbell, in the mid-sixteenth century. Or take the Lament for Iain Garbh macGille Chaluim of Raasay, drowned in 1671:

> Nochd gur h-ìosal do chluasag,
> fo lic fhuaraidh na tuinne,
> 's ann an clachan na traghad
> tha mo ghràdh-sa 'na uirigh.
>
> Lowly to-night is thy pillow,
> cold billows thy tomb-stone,
> graveyard of the shore at ebb
> is the bed of my adored one.

The great age, however, of Scottish Gaelic poetry is (so far) the eighteenth century, with its greatest figure in Alexander Macdonald, Alasdair MacMhaighstir Alasdair (*c.* 1700-70). Son of an Episcopalian minister, of the Clanranald branch of the clan, partly educated at Glasgow University, by turns schoolmaster, catechist and farmer, Episcopalian, Presbyterian and Papist, he was above all a nationalist and a Jacobite, serving in the campaign to Culloden and pouring out martial incitements. His greatest piece is *The Birlinn of Clanranald*, describing the voyage of a chief's galley across the Minch as if it were going from Heaven to Hell and back, with a range of rhythm and harmony and sensibility unparalleled in any tone-poem. Hugh MacDiarmid's rhymed version in English has been widely admired, and thought to convey the impression of a tremendous and unique work; but even this excellent attempt bears hardly more relation to the original Gaelic than the view of the stained glass from out-side bears to the sensation of gazing up from inside the Sainte Chapelle. Macdonald's extant work, a minor part of his whole output, has a con-siderable range—amatory, satirical, descriptive and didactic—everywhere challenging for the command of language. *The Sugar-Brook*, for instance, conveys melodiously the whole succession of seasonal pictures arising around a farm he had. *The Praise of Mòrag* and the pair of lengthy pieces on summer and winter combine remarkably direct utterance and *tours de force*. Always popular, though his more Rabelaisian pieces have had their detractors, he is also a poets' poet, without rival in Gaelic till the present generation.

Colonel John Roy Stewart (1700-52) is another picturesque Jacobite militant, equally fiery with sword and pen, who died in French exile. John MacCodrum (1693-1779) and Rob Donn Mackay (1714-78) are best remembered for their satires, and William Ross (1762-90) for love-lyrics and pastoral pieces. Of the hymn-writers, far the most powerful was Dugald Buchanan (1716-68). To outsiders savouring the melodies of Gaelic verse without too deep an interest in its subjects, Duncan Bàn Macintyre (1724-1812) has a great deal to offer, especially in his *Praise of Ben Dorain*, whose movements imitate the variations of a pibroch, while a wealth of epithets is lavished on every aspect of his favourite mountain.

Among nineteenth-century poets one may mention Ewen Maclachlan (1775-1822), with his pieces on the four seasons; Evan MacColl, Dr John Maclachlan, Dugald Macphail, Mrs Mary Mackellar, Neil Macleod and Mrs Mary Macpherson; but they all tend to show the mid-Victorian senti-mentality and pretty-prettiness. Most high-flying was William Livingstone (1808-70), with saga-style pieces on historical and political themes. The Barra playwright Donald Sinclair (1886-1932) wrote some verses of merit, and singable ditties and satires continued to appear during the first third of the twentieth century.

The 1930s then threw up two major Gaelic poets, Sorley Maclean from Raasay (*b.* 1911) and George Campbell Hay from Tarbert, Loch Fyne (*b*. 1915). To colloquial and scholarly command of the whole resources of Gaelic each of them joins a contemporary sensibility, conversant with the themes of the international *avant-garde* and deeply obsessed not only with personal problems but with the great national and world challenges of our time. In *Seventeen Poems for Sixpence* (1940), a joint pamphlet with Robert Garioch, Maclean came to grips not only with the vicissitudes of a lover but with the implications of the Spanish Civil War. In *Dàin do Eimhir* (1943) we had many love-poems of great subtlety and perceptiveness, akin to much of Donne or Valéry; as well as magnificent descriptive pieces and keen-cutting epigrams. Not yet published in full is the great *An Cuilithionn*, where the history and struggles of the Skye crofters are portrayed along with the world-historical development of which they are a microcosm; and all this in a superb gamut of verse-forms and diction.

George Hay is a versatile linguist and a master-craftsman in Gaelic most of all, though he has written poems that sing themselves as you read in other tongues also, Scots, English, French, Norse, for instance; and has made admirable verse-translations from ancient and modern Greek, Serbo-Croat, Arabic, Italian, Welsh and so on (*Fuaran Sleibh*, 1948; *Wind on Loch Fyne*, 1948; *O na Ceithir Airdean*, 1952). Many of these pieces are, of course, skilful literary exercises, which nevertheless have a value beyond themselves in enriching the expressive powers of the language; but Hay has given us also plenty of poems of the fullest power on a wide range of themes, from a Highland mother's lullaby to a stark portrayal of an air raid on Bizerta.

Some very interesting new lines in Gaelic verse were opened up by Derick Thomson from Lewis (*b*. 1922) in *An Dealbh Briste* (1950), showing again the combination of scholarly command of language with a modern sensibility and individual power of expression. Here is another indication that, though the colloquial basis of Gaelic in the population is still declining through inimical economic and social factors, the poetic tradition retains a certain life and is able to branch out in new directions. After all, Gaelic is a superb instrument for poetry, long fallow, but with great latent fertility. With current and impending stirrings of the Scottish national consciousness who can foresee what fresh force may be springing from these ancient roots, just as Hebrew, so long a fossilized and hieratic language, has renewed its social vitality and given birth to powerful poetry?

SELECT BIBLIOGRAPHY

Sàr-Obair nam Bàrd Gaelach: or, The Beauties of Gaelic Poetry, ed. John Mackenzie, 1841 (new edition, 1907).

Gaelic Bards, 1411-1715 and 1715-1765, ed. A. Maclean Sinclair, 1890.

Nigel MacNeill, *The Literature of the Highlanders*, 1898.

Songs of Duncan MacIntyre, ed. G. Calder, 1912. In Gaelic and English.

The Poems of Alexander Macdonald (MacMhaighstir Alasdair), with metrical translations by A. Macdonald of Killearnan and A. Macdonald of Kiltarlity, 1924.

Ortha nan Gaidheal: Carmina Gadelica, ed. Alexander Carmichael, 5 vols., 1928-54. With parallel translations.

Bardachd Ghàidhlig: Specimens of Gaelic Poetry, ed. W. J. Watson, 1932.

The Owl Remembers, ed. J. Mackechnie and P. McGlynn, 1932. An anthology with parallel versions.

Highland Songs of the Forty-Five, ed. John Lorne Campbell, 1933. With translations and a valuable introduction.

The Poems of Mary Macleod, ed. J. Carmichael Watson, 1934. With translations.

Dàin do Eimhir, with some English versions by the author, Somhairle MacGhillEathain (Sorley Maclean), 1943.

Fuaran Sleibh, with English translations by the author, George Campbell Hay, 1948.

The Scottish Gaelic Text Society's editions of John MacCodrum, Duncan Macintyre and others. In progress: with parallel translations.

Selections from *An Cuilithionn*, with parallel translations, by Sorley Maclean, 1955 (in *Lines Review*, vii; 33 Marchmont Road, Edinburgh 9).

From My Scottish Diary

During the years 1950-60 Douglas contributed an article thrice
weekly to the *News Chronicle*, of which the following three are
typical.

FIRST FOOT GETS FIRST SOAKING

SURVIVAL OF DOCUMENTS through the ages has hitherto been largely haphazard.

A scrap of a mummy wrapping from an Egyptian tomb may give us our only glimpse of the life and activities of a certain section of humanity over many centuries.

Supposing a catastrophe of civilisation that destroyed all the files of the *News Chronicle Dispatch*, and all twentieth-century Scottish records, except a news cutting of the little piece I am now typing, the historian a couple of millennia hence might have to make do with so scanty a document for his magnum opus on the way in which the Scottish provincial intelligentsia brought in the New Year of 1957.

I wish him joy of it, and set down some details with all sobriety.

The chimes of midnight having sounded for the end of Hogmanay Part I, the family, gathered at the open front door (old Scottish custom), greeted one another with a babel of conventional exclamations and osculations.

There then appeared one whom Alastair Borthwick's Islay neighbours would consider properly dressed, a Tory town councillor whose hip was equipped with a blend of native distillations from barley.

He was shortly followed by a Labour town councillor, similarly furnished.

The two gentlemen had been in dispute in public, both being dissatisfied about the raising of municipal rents.

The one because they were raised too little, the other because they were raised at all. However, in private, the first and second foots raised their glasses in cordial wishes for 1957.

Various callers and beverages having been dealt with, somewhat after 2 a.m., the Scottish provincial intelligentsia retired to sleep, the front door bell being disconnected.

Waking at seven, I drank tea and looked at Otto Demus's thick book on the Norman Mosaics of Sicily, and the Skira publication on Byzantine painting.

Passing to coffee and Euripides' Hippolytus, I roused my spouse about noon, and we went to first foot our next-door neighbour, the Rev. Erskine Stewart.

Traditionally, a black-bearded man is a lucky first foot, and I offered an oatcake, a peat, and a small bottle of cherry brandy from Copenhagen.

The Minister reciprocated with Calvados, the firewater distilled by the Bretons from cider.

After these international touches, my wife consulted Mrs Stewart, a globe-trotting lady who can even speak so outlandish a tongue as Czech, and who collects cookery books of various nations. The topic was sauces for pheasants.

The Minister lent me James Fisher's recent book on Rockall, in which I was delighted to find that in 1696 the hospitable folk of St Kilda were strict observers of the Sabbath, and forbade the repair of their boat on a Sunday by a party of French and Spanish sailors shipwrecked on Rockall.

To help down the roast pheasant, we had that Latian wine of Monte-fiascone named Est Est Est, from the trebled enthusiasm of the servant of a travelling ecclesiastic who wanted written on the tavern doors whether there was good drinking inside.

High tide being about 3 p.m., I took my first dip of the year in the river Tay, no colder than in May, and ten degrees warmer than the biting easterly gale.

The beach was deserted but for a septuagenarian lady artist, Mrs Mabel McGeorge. A hardy Victorian, she was enjoying, as she said, the pounding of the waves on the shore.

. . . Here the document breaks off, and the historian is left to imagine the rest of the Ne'er Day celebration characteristic of Scottish intellectuals in 1957.

THIS WAS NO BURNS SUPPER—FOR A' THAT

TELEVISION VIEWERS must have derived very queer ideas of our traditional Burns Supper from the glimpses they were vouchsafed of a function I attended the other night in Edinburgh.

It was the inaugural celebration by something called the B.B.C. Television Burns Club, and was enjoyable, in spite of certain disconcerting features that might have made Scotia's Bard turn in his grave and reach for his satirical pen.

Since Burns was a poet, a fact too often forgotten at Burns Suppers, the organisers had mobilised a scattering of versifiers, headed by Hugh MacDiarmid, wearing a tartan tie.

Sydney Goodsir Smith had excavated from his grandfather's bottom drawer a superb Victorian waistcoat of watered silk, and flourished a monocle with an authentic air.

A selection of the public had balloted for the hundred or so dinner places in the studio, and paid 12s. 6d. a head for the pleasure of eating haggis beneath a top table graced by various leaders of the arts, the Burns Federation, and so on.

The poets, Norman MacCaig, Robert Kemp, Alexander Scott, and the rest, were imported merely as rustics haggis-fed to be picked out for an instant by the TV cameras.

But the actual performing was done by others.

And some singular performing we had. A B.B.C. elocutionist in a dinner-jacket stood up and read out the poem about a man being a man for a' that.

"What though on hamely fare we dine, wear hodden gray, and a' that?"

Not only was the tuxedo not hodden gray, but the recital was performed much in the manner of a Tory Parliamentary Secretary drooling out the last pages of a departmental brief.

Still stranger was the mode of addressing the haggis.

Bamboozled no doubt by the TV cameras, the reciter got his lines mixed up and lost some of them, then drew a tremendous Highland dirk, encrusted with huge Cairngorms, and did some bayonet practice on a truly colossal haggis.

After which, to everyone's amazement, he grasped the billowing haggis in both hands and punched it so that the contents tumbled out.

All this took place after we had in fact finished our supper and the cutlery had been cleared, so that the viewers could see nothing but glasses and whisky bottles on the tablecloth.

Sassenachs who formerly believed that a haggis was something Scotsmen wear with the kilt will now conjecture that it is a curiously shaped sack of porridge which we eat with our hands.

Burns would have been more at home with the Rotary Club of Cowdenbeath whose annual celebration I attended a night or two before, in the heart of the West Fife coalfield.

I never heard more genuinely Scots singing than there, the songs being pronounced with perfect truth and naturalness by singers who speak the old Scots every day.

Particularly fine was a young man who works as a fitter about the pits, George Eggo.

But others who lacked the natural good voice still made up with the right spirit.

And I liked the homespun kindly bluntness of a voter of thanks to the artists, who commented on the execution of "Willie brewed a peck o maut" by a fraternity known as The Terrible Trio.

He said, "They really made a valiant effort, but their musical knowledge is lower than mine."

Genuine Burnsians, the Rotarians gave me five guineas as a donation to the Scottish National Dictionary, an object which the Bard would much have approved.

I left Cowdenbeath station at dawn, with a prospect of the moon, in its last phase, spelling C for Cowdenbeath, standing above a charming composition of a gasometer and a pit-bing with an intriguing silhouette. The burgh lacks amenity, but I took kindly to the burghers.

NOW THE RUSSIANS MAY TRY TO
LAUNCH RABBIE

RUSSIANS, IN THE INTERVALS of sending rockets moonwards, may be making a film about Robert Burns, if negotiations go well.

They have been initiated by Mr Alex McCrindle, Scottish secretary of the British Actors' Equity Association, with Samuel Yakovlevitch Marshak, who won a Stalin prize for turning a lot of Burns's poems into Russian.

At the same time as I learn of this move, I receive from Warsaw an elegant volume of verse translations of Burns into Polish, by four hands, edited by Dr Alexander Krynski, a graduate of St Andrews and Oxford.

I cannot cope with Polish, but my colleague Dr Stan Seliga, a learned

98

Pole, tells me Burns has gone extremely well into his native tongue, and that the two lady translators have not shrunk from turning what he calls "very drastic" bits of Burns into very drastic Polish.

In the same week arrives a request from Mr Hugh Martin, editor of Esperanto En Skotlando, for a bicentenary article on some international aspect of Burns, to circulate the globe in Esperanto.

Against this background I am trying to assess the merits of the controversy the poet Norman McCaig has set flaring by a speech at the Newbattle Abbey Adult Education College, where he advanced the proposition that, though Burns was a great poet, Hugh MacDiarmid is a greater poet.

Hugh MacDiarmid modestly accepts this McCaig tribute as a mere matter of course, and launches out on a new tack in addressing the Rotary Club of Carnoustie.

Schools, thinks MacDiarmid, are wrong in starting by teaching the great poets of the past. He thinks they ought to begin with contemporary poets whose subject matter corresponds to issues that are very much in the air.

MacDiarmid's idea of an issue being very much in the air is to publish in 1957 a polemical poem against the late Roy Campbell's book, Flowering Rifle, in which that South African Scot took a pro-Franco line on the Spanish Civil War of 20 years ago.

MacDiarmid also recommends people to read William Dunbar as Scotland's greatest poet, not Burns, which would take us the best part of three centuries further back out of our glorious contemporary era.

McCaig's specific charges are five: that Burns's scope was narrow, his intelligence not large, his imaginative grasp superficial; he was not a great craftsman; and he could never make up his mind whether to write in Scots or English.

Considering Burns died at 37, his scope was comparable to the range of MacDiarmid's interests in poetry, especially when we recall how sciences and techniques and political movements have developed with increasing speed since 1796.

Burns's contemporaries, such as Prof. Dugald Stewart, testified with surprise that he could hold his own intellectually in any company, at a time when Edinburgh was in the first flight as an intellectual centre.

Carlyle long ago pointed out defects in Burns's craftsmanship, but MacDiarmid's is even more defective.

Where MacDiarmid scores is in imaginative power, whether in Scots or English or the multilingual medium he attempts.

His vision is wider than Burns's, but not more intense where elemental and permanent human relations and feelings are concerned.

MacDiarmid, great poet as he has been in his best work, is unlikely to be other than a poets' poet, and what Shakespeare called caviar to the general, even if served up with a drappie of Soviet vodka.

Burns, in whatever tongue translated, goes on speaking to the heart of many in all generations. And the heart aye 's the pairt aye that maks us richt or wrang.

McCaig's preoccupation with image-manipulation seems to have blinded him to the great poetic potency of heartfelt direct utterance, where Burns is a great master.

From *The Burdies*

A translation of Aristophanes' *Birds*, presented in the Lyceum
Theatre, Edinburgh, during the 1966 Festival. This is the parabasis
of the chorus, lines 676-800.

CHORUS: C'wa nou, darlin wi swack broun limbs,
    aye the dearest o burds tae me,
    ye accompany aa my hymns,
    nichtigal, wi your melodie.
    Ye're here, ye're here, a joy tae see;
    unco bonnie the voice ye bring.
    Blythelie nou, wi your flute sae clear,
    lat the music o spring ootring,
    and stert the anapaests here.

Coryphaeus: Nou listen, ye humans, wi dowf dreich lifes,
    like the leafs i their brief generations,
    ye shaidawy fushionless clans that are made
    oot o cley like a patter's creations,
    puir wingless mannies that last but a day,
    dream-phantoms, miserable craturs:
    nou tak tent til us, that are skaithless o daith,
    wi our indestructible naturs,
    etherial, heivenly, free frae auld age,
    and wyce wi our science eternal:
    we'll learn you the lear o ilk thing i the air
    and the cosmic system supernal:
    us burds, and the gods, aa the rivers, the Mirk,
    and Chaos, wi true erudition,
    whan ye ken hou it aa cam tae be ye'll condemn
    auld Darwin tae endless perdition.
    Nou at first there was Chaos and Nicht, and the Mirk,
    and Tartarus spelderan fozy:
    nae yirth and nae air, nae heiven was there,
    till at last, i the infinit bosie
    o the pitblack Mirk the dark-wingit Nicht
    lay a wind-egg, airest o onie,
    frae whilk, as the times cam roond, there sprang
    the Love-God, Eros, sae bonny,

wi his spauls bricht sheenan wi twa gowd wings,
and a luik like the stormwinds dizzy.
Ae nicht i the braidness of Tartarus syne
the Love-God and Chaos gat busy,
and cleckit us, fedderit race of the burds,
first species he brocht up hither:
for the breed o Immortals didna exist
till Love jyned aathing wi ither;
syne mixter-maxter, the wey they were jyned,
cam Heiven and Ocean thegither,
and Yirth, and the daithless gods, ilk ane,
the hale blest clan. Sae ye see nou
us burds is the auldest Immortals o aa.
Frae a feck o pruifs ye'll agree nou
we're the Love-God's clan. For we're fleean aye,
and wi lovers we're aye consortan:
there's a wheen bonny boys that was wearyit o their ploys
at the term o sic callants' sportin,
yet throu our pouer and chairm they hae gane airm in airm
wi their auld bosom frien for a dander;
juist a quail or a coot can win owre a wee brute,
or a cockerel or aiblins a gander.
The best o the boons ye mortals may win,
it's til us, the burds, that ye awe them.
Think first o the winter, the spring, and the hairst,—
sic saisons aa, we shaw them.
It's the time for tae saw whan awa tae Africaa
the crane wi a caa gaes wingan;
then the maister o a ship suld dover by the fire,
wi his rudder i the boatshed hingan.
Gie a coat til the bauld Teddy boy gin he's cauld,
lest he tirr ye, wi 's bike-cheen swingan.
I the spring whan ye see the gled hawk flee,
ye'll ken that the simmer maun follow,
wi the clippin o the oo frae the yowes on the knowes;
and ye'll learn frae the flicht o the swallow
ye may sell your duffle coat, and buy a baithin suit.
Sae we are your Phoebus Apollo,
the god o prophecie. We're your oracles and shrines:

ye aye turn first til us burdies,
as til Ammon or Dodona or the Delphic voice.
Ye're gleg for tae speir what our word is,
gin ye ettle tae trade or try fuitbaa pools,
and whiles gin ye want tae get mairryit.
"*A wee burdie tellt me,*" ye aften explain;
and an omen straucht ye declare it
gin ocht that 's uncannie and orra befaas.
Sic omens are monie and varyit,—
a pun or a sneeze, or a servant ye meet,
or a cuddie that gies a bit nicker.
Sae we are your Phoebus Apollo, the god
whas prophecies aa are aye siccar.
Nou gin ye revere us burds as divine,
like prophetess Muses we'll gie ye a sign,
o the winds and the weather, the simmer sae braw,
and winter and drouth. But we'll no rin awa
and sit i the cloods wi our neb i the air
the wey Zeus hunkers and glowers up there.
But we'll byde wi you, and we'll gie ye aye,
you and your bairns, and their bairns forbye,
walth and guid halth, lang life and peace,
youth and lauchter, and dances and feasts,
doos' milk and burds' custard, till ye may staw
wi the rowth we'll gie ye o aa things braw:
sae walthy ye'll be, ane and aa.

CHORUS: Muse o the wuidland,
tiotio tiotio tioteenx,
braikit burd, wi you I'm hiddlan
in dens or on muntainy ballochs,
tiotio tioteenx,
set i the reeshilan hair o the sallochs,
tiotio tioteenx;
and frae my swack broun hause I poor
sangs for Pan in a halie shouer,
and solemn dansetunes for the Muntain Mither,
tototo tototo totototeenx.
As a bee that flits i the heather

103

Thorpe Davie has soukit the frute frae me
o his daithless sangs' sweet melodie,
tiotio tioteenx.

Coryphaeus: Nou, spectators, gin there's onie
    wants tae weave a cantie life
mang the burdies for the future,
    straucht aff lat him come til us.
What they damn as crimes in Embro,
    strang forbidden by the Law,
here wi us amang the burdies
    aa sic deeds are braw and richt.
Here by statute it's illegal
    for tae gie your dad a clour;
thonder that's aaricht wi us,
    gin onie chiel rins at his dad,
dunts him sair, and says "Come on.
    Pit up your spur gin ye wad fecht."
Aiblins ane o ye's a Paddie,
    tattooed wi the shamrock green;
here amang us, fegs, they'll caa him
    juist a braikit paiterick.
Aiblins ane o ye's a Welsher,
    juist as bad as Taffie Jones;
mang the burds he'll be a chaffie,
    o the breed that nibbles leeks.
Aiblins ane o ye's a Cohen,
    frae the tribe o Israel;
lat him sproot heraldic plumage,
    syne he'll be a real Colquhoun.
Aiblins Paisias' son, the feartie,
    plans tae gie the castle yetts
tae the riffraff; sae we'll ken him
    for a quail, his daddie's chick,
sin amang the burds it isna
    shame tae flichter like a quail.

CHORUS: Swans o Apollo,
    tiotio tiotio tioteenx,

soondan oot their wingbeats hollow,
adored him wi dunneran clamour,
tiotio tioteenx,
sattlan by Hebrus, the river o glamour,
tiotio tioteenx,
and throu the cloods their clangour rowed;
braikit clans o beasts were cowed;
the windless heiven lowned the laigh waves under;
tototo tototo totototeenx.
then Olympus echoed the dunder;
the gods were bumbazed, but the Muses' thrang
wi the Graces jyned took up the sang,
tiotio tioteenx.

Coryphaeus: Naething's better, naething's nicer
    than tae grow a pair o wings.
Juist imagine, you spectators,
    gin ye had the pouer o flicht.
Syne gin onie ane was hungry,
    fashed wi tragic choruses,
fleean aff he'd airt for hame
    and tak a richt guid herty lunch;
then, wi weel-swalled kyte belyve,
    licht doun again amang ye here.
Aiblins ane, like Patrocleides,
    wants tae gae whaur Charlemagne
coudna send a deputy;
    wi wings he needna fyle his breeks;
he'd flee awa and ease hissel,
    and syne he'd flee doun here again.
Aiblins ane o ye is busy
    wi some houghmagandie ploy,
syne he sees the wifie's hubbie
    sittan i the Council seats,
sae he gies his wings a heeze,
    and aff he flees abuin your heids;
whan he's had his pleisur thonder,
    back he comes and doucely sits.
Siccar, it fair cowes the cuddie

juist tae hae the pouer o flicht.
See Dieitrephes the merchant,
    him that sells wee wingit quaichs,—
first he's Colonel o the Horse Guairds,
    and he cocks his bunnet braw;
neist the cockie horsecock rides
    his cockhorse as a Brigadier.

Miltonic Light on Professor Denys Page's Homeric Theory

This essay, which first appeared in the academic periodical *Greece and Rome,* Second Series, Vol. VI, No. 1 in March 1956, is a refutation of the theory that the *Iliad* and the *Odyssey* were by different authors. The article is full of wit and by its reductio ad absurdum gave much amusement to the Classical world.

IN HIS SPRIGHTLY VOLUME *The Homeric Odyssey* (Clarendon Press, Oxford, 1955; originally the Mary Flexner Lectures at Bryn Mawr College, Pennsylvania), Professor Denys Page favoured the public with what he terms (p. 149) a few points of interest from his notes on the vocabularies of the *Iliad* and the *Odyssey*. Listing words and phrases found in the *Iliad* but rarely or never in the *Odyssey*, and vice versa, he concludes (p. 157) "that the two poems were composed and transmitted in separate regions of Hellas."

If Professor Page's statistical presuppositions and inferences be valid for the Homeric poems, they should apply with equal force to comparable bodies of verse. Accordingly, it seemed worth while to investigate what light his criteria might shed on the epics and other poetic works ascribed to John Milton, and to observe in turn whether the Miltonic study might reflect any light, or even "darkness visible," on his theory about the *Odyssey.*

Some of the Homeric words and phrases examined are classed by Professor Page as traditional archaic terms of Epic vocabulary; others are listed as "generally serviceable" terms that remained common in all later Greek literature; a third group consists of relatively modern words that allegedly made their way into the original *Iliad* and *Odyssey* through recitations by generations of rhapsodes in separate regions of Hellas. Professor Page argues repeatedly against the ascription to mere chance of the occurrence of a particular word in the *Iliad* and not in the *Odyssey*, or vice versa; he insists that the two poems "were largely created by persons possessed of two divergent stocks of phrases," and were transmitted by persons "who differed at least in respect of what was deemed admissible in Epic verse" (p. 157). Yet he nowhere discusses fundamentally the calculus of probabilities involved in all this. Indeed, it is not an easy matter to reduce to logic or mathematics; for which very reason a succinct application of Professor Page's criteria to Milton may be a speedier method of illuminating the play of chance in the occurrence of single words in different verse compositions.

The bulk of the Miltonic poems in English is rather less than that of the Homeric epics, but their vocabulary not very significantly less. John Bradshaw's *A Concordance to the Poetical Works of John Milton* (Swan Sonnenschein, London, 1894) covers all the English verse ascribed to Milton except the metrical versions of the psalms of David and the translations in the prose works. (The Pagean arguments obviously put out of court *ab limine* the fantastic ascription to the same John Milton of writings in Greek, Latin, and Italian.) The miscellaneous English poems (*Lycidas, Comus*, &c.) come to 2,620 lines, written at various dates, mostly before *Paradise Lost*. Adding them to *Paradise Regained* (2,070 lines) and *Samson Agonistes* (1,758), both written later, one finds a total of 6,448 lines to set against the 10,558 lines of *Paradise Lost*, hereinafter referred to compendiously as *Plo*. Let the smaller corpus of Miltonic verse be termed *Min(ora)*. The proportion of *Min* to *Plo* is reasonably comparable to that of the *Odyssey* (12,110 lines in the Oxford text) to the *Iliad* (15,693). *Min* is 61 per cent. of *Plo* in size, the *Odyssey* 77 per cent. of the *Iliad*. Bradshaw's *Concordance* purports to give all the words except some pronouns, conjunctions, adverbs, and prepositions; but in these categories he states that "any of those used peculiarly are given." On the basis of a 10 per cent. sample count I reckon the Miltonic stock of words at some 8,000, as against some 9,000 for the *Iliad* and *Odyssey* together, calculated from 10 per cent. sample counts in H. Ebeling's *Lexicon Homericum* (Teubner, Leipzig, 1880), with subtraction of the 763 words peculiar to the *Homeric Hymns* (as listed with asterisks in Index I to *The Homeric Hymns*, edited by T. W. Allen, W. R. Halliday, and E. E. Sikes, 2nd ed., Oxford, 1936). This calculation tallies closely with another made by a 10 per cent. sampling in R. J. Cunliffe's *A Lexicon of the Homeric Dialect* (Blackie, London and Bombay, 1924). Those concerned with a calculus of probabilities may note that *Min*, with 6,448 lines, is rather more than half as long as the *Odyssey*, with 12,110.

Professor Page draws particular attention to two single words, φλόξ and ποινή, the alleged non-occurrence of which in the *Odyssey*, while they are common in the *Iliad*, seems to him "to preclude all but the remotest possibility that mere chance might be the cause of this remarkable by-passing of the *Odyssey*" (pp. 152–3). ποινή occurs ten times in the *Iliad*, never in the *Odyssey* (for he excludes *Od*. xxiii. 312, where we find

108

ποινή, because he considers *Od.* xxiii from 297 on as "the Continuation"). At the same time Professor Page notes that the *Odyssey* uses νήποινος (eight times, in fact), a word not found in the *Iliad.* Now it is worth observing that the word *penalty* occurs eight times in *Plo* but not once in *Min.* Will Professor Page ascribe this to mere chance? Or will he contend that the author of *Min*, being different in time and place from the author of *Plo*, did not know the word *penalty*, just as the concocter (or concocters) and transmitters of the *Odyssey* did not know its Greek equivalent?

Professor Page makes much of the word φλόξ, as being the common Greek word for the flame of fire. It is used nineteen times in the *Iliad*, but not once in the *Odyssey*, according to him (p. 152). He overlooks *Od.* xxiv. 71, where it occurs. He also lists some words from the same root (φλόξ) that occur in the *Iliad* but not in the *Odyssey*; and I add to his list the actual number of their occurrences: φλογέος, 2; ζαφλεγής, 1; φλέγμα, 1; φλέγω, 2; φλεγέθω, 4; ἐπιφλέγω, 2; καταφλέγω, 1. Professor Page contends that there are "two theoretically possible reasons" for the absence of φλόξ and its fellows from the *Odyssey.* Either the root was wholly unknown to the Odyssean poet, or its non-occurrence was mere chance. And, he asks, how likely is that chance? One might begin by insisting that φλόξ in fact occurs at *Od.* xxiv. 71, which Professor Page has no adequate ground for rejecting.[1] Secondly, one might compare the occurrence of the same common serviceable word φλόξ in Aeschylus: five times in the *P.V.*, four in the *Agamemnon*, once each in the *Persai* and *Choephoroi*; never at all in three out of the seven extant plays of Aeschylus; and once in a fragment (*Fr.* 300). In other words, the incidence of φλόξ in Aeschylus is very much like its incidence in Homer, absent from roughly half the corpus. In Euripides φλόξ occurs fifteen times in four plays (*Bakchai, Helene, Ion, Troiades*); fifteen times in another twelve of the extant plays; and never at all in three (*H.F., Hippolytos, Orestes*), but five times in fragments.

It may be mere chance that φλόξ occurs nineteen times in the *Iliad*, and only once in the *Odyssey*, just as it is mere chance that the two occurrences of φλέγω are both in the same book of the *Iliad* (xxi. 13, 365). The four occurrences of φλεγέθω are all in the last third of the *Iliad.* Why not in Books i–xvi? Will Professor Page tell us they are by a different author in a different region?

It is curious that in Milton *fire* is always singular in *Min*, while the

---

[1] I am not convinced by his chapter V. Homer could not leave his hero in an unsettled blood-feud.

plural, *fires*, occurs thirteen times in *Plo*. Of other words relating to fire, *Plo* has *empyreal* eleven times, *empyrean* once, both of which are unknown to *Min*. These distributions may be ascribed to mere chance, as also the occurrence of *infinite* twenty-three times in *Plo*, with the adverb *infinitely* and the noun *infinitude* twice each. *Min* has none of them. Would Professor Page argue that *Plo* and *Min* must be ascribed to different authors? How does he account for the fact that *Plo* uses the noun *substance* fourteen times, and the adjective *substantial* and the adverb *substantially*, while *Min* knows them all not? Why should *Plo* use *horns* only in the plural, four times, while *Min* has only the singular *horn*, found six times?

Professor Page asks the learned public (p. 164, n. 21), "Does anybody believe that it is *by mere chance* that neither of the [Homeric] Epics employs κίνδυνος, μόχθος, νόμος [and νομίζω], ὀργή, σεμνός, τύνη, φέγγος?" Among straightforward English translations of those Greek words, Milton lacks *risk, statute, enact, propensity, temperament, revered,* and *august*. What conclusion can be drawn from this Miltonic lack? None.

Among words of the Miltonic corpus why should *Plo* alone use *claim* (11 times), *depart* (9), *discourse* (as noun, 11), *ensue* (11), *hiss* (8), *knee* (7), *original* (7), *ourselves* (9), *pit* (7), *purge* (8), *rebellious* (9), *swim* (9), *tent* (10, usually in the plural), *war* (as verb, 7 times)? Because it happened to suit him in *Paradise Lost* and not elsewhere.

To list further words found five times or more, is it mere chance that *Plo* alone uses *angry, Apostate, apply, behest, beware, cattle, circumference, confirm, contrive, darken, dawning, delightful, desolate, dewy, discord, dissolution, distemper, diurnal, Dominations, elect* (participle as adjective), *encamp, equally, escape* (verb), *exhalation, foreknowledge, forewarn, fragrance, hemisphere, hoarse, hot, ice, immediate, impossible, impress, interrupt, laugh* (noun), *myriads, odious, Omnipotent, ours, patriarch, populous, proper, prosper, rational, reside, retreat, righteousness, sanctity, satiate, shrub, skirt, stature, theirs, to and fro, visible, waist*?

Consider next a few of the vocables exclusive to *Min*. On what calculus of mere chance is the word *lady* used twenty-one times in *Min*, but never in *Plo*, if the same John Milton wrote them both? It looks as if we may have to postulate a Deutero-Milton, who in turn might be analysable into a Protero-Deutero-Milton and a Hystero-Deutero-Milton, an analysis to be recommended to the transatlantic Ph.D. industry. Professor Page, diligent as he is in assembling lists of words exclusive to the *Iliad* or to the *Odyssey*, will be prompt to observe whatever arcane significance may lie in the fact that *Min* has exclusive use of such miscellaneous words as *masters* (5 occurrences), *swains* (12), *schools* (5), *spells* (13), *fortune(s)* (8), *chastity* (7), *asses* (6), *tomb* (6), *eyesight* (5), *forty* (6), *aged* (5), *ne'er* (5), *nurse* (as verb, 8), *pull* (6), *rob* (3), *robber* (3), *sheen* (4), *sheeny*, *trim* (5), *very* (4).

To list only words occurring at least thrice in *Plo*, why, in *Min*, did the Deutero-Milton not use such generally serviceable common English terms as the following?

Afraid, agony, angry, ardour, askance, attentive, beauteous, belch, bland, bog, boundless, brink, casual, commotion, compute, conscious, convex, covet, crowd, dalliance, deceit, deluge, demeanour, desolate, difficulty, dilated, dimension, disclose, discord, dislike, dislodge, doubled, downy, drown, eccentric, eminence, enormous, equality, equinoctial, erroneous, exile, familiar, fan, florid, fluid, fruitless, glide, harden, havoc, hew, imminent, immortality, incapable, incur, indignation, infuse, inoffensive, insect, instant, intellectual, intercept, intricate, introduce, irksome, lamb, largely, longitude, lop, male, manifold, material, meridian, mitigate, nimble, nourishment, opprobrious, paternal, pavement, pendent, phalanx, plague, plunge, prostrate, push, rapid, reflect, refuge, reluctant, remedy, rend, resplendent, revisit, sidelong, slime, slink, sloth, spouse, stranger, swerve, sympathy, tempestuous, terrestrial, tolerable, torrid, type, unfeigned, unspeakable, uproar, vigilance, wonderful.

On the principles of reasoning applied by Professor Page to Homeric vocabulary, one must conclude that the Deutero-Milton who wrote *Min* lived in a region of the English language isolated from the speech-area of the genuine original John Milton to whom *Plo* is ascribed. It is odd that *Min* alone refers, and that twice, to a place called Cambridge. On which side of the Atlantic this must be sought remains to be inquired.

Now proof in these matters is cumulative. I spare the reader the lengthy lists of nouns and adjectives exclusive to *Plo* or to *Min*, which I drew up from Bradshaw's *Concordance*, and the shorter lists of adverbs, of which some three dozen are found only in *Plo* and about as many in *Min* alone. To confine our attention to verbs, the following lists, while not exhaustive, are much longer than the exclusive lists of verbs cited by Professor Page in respect of the *Iliad* and the *Odyssey*, and any proof drawn from them is *pro tanto* the more cogent.

Plo uses, and *Min* does not use, the following verbs:

abolish, abound, alter, amuse, annex, applaud, apply, arraign, asperse,

111

*attach, balance, belch, bellow, besmear, bestir, beware, blush, bray,
calculate, cancel, cavil, champ, circumscribe, cite, claim, clash, compute,
concoct, concur, condense, confide, confirm, congregate, contribute,
contrive, convey, correspond, covet, cringe, culminate, dandle, darken,
debar, deface, deflower, deify, delineate, depart, detect, deter, dig, digest,
dilate, disagree, disclose, dislike, dislodge, disorder, dissent, dissuade,
double, drown, emulate, encamp, ensure, escape, exhale, falter, foment,
forewarn, glide, gnaw, harden, harness, hew, hiss, imply, impress, incur,
inhabit, intercept, interrupt, introduce, laugh, lick, lop, mitigate, oblige,
pave, plunge, prop, propagate, prosper, prune, purge, push, reflect,
reform, relax, reside, retreat, satiate, scoff, scribble, slink, spill, spout,
starve, struggle, stumble, stun, suit, swerve, swim, veer, wade, wage,
wallow, war, winnow, wreak, writhe, yawn.*

Verbs found in *Min*, but unknown to, or eschewed by, *Plo*, include
the following, of varying degrees of commonness and utility:

*assuage, aver, avow, baffle, baulk, bawl, befriend, blab, brew, budge,
carve, censure, chafe, challenge, chant, chat, cheat, chide, clatter, cleanse,
clip, condole, confute, congeal, contradict, crawl, cull, daunt, define, dis-
approve, discomfit, dodge, doff, fester, fetter, grapple, grudge, hammer,
hamper, harass, hoard, hug, hum, knock, lock, moan, nod, nurse, peep,
peer, perch, pick, prance, print, pull, quarrel, rankle, requite, rig, rob,
score, scramble, sell, shove, shriek, sift, sip, slake, slit, sneeze, soak, span,
stare, straggle, strut, sweep, sympathize, tan, tax, tease, thatch, throttle,
trap, tug, tumble, twist, vomit, wail, warrant, waver, waylay, weave,
whet, whirl, whistle, wink, wreck, wrench, wring.*

Let that suffice for proof based on merely numerical data, on the
occurrence or non-occurrence of single words. It will be clear to Professor Page and others holding the principles of the *Chorizontes* that
Milton is at least as liable to fission as Homer. Even more revealing, in
our age of archaeological television "stars," may be an excursion into the
archaeological implications of the exclusive vocabularies of *Plo* and *Min*.
We may begin with the fauna and flora mentioned.

The *Plo* folk's *cattle* are referred to no fewer than seven times, and we
are not surprised to find exclusive to them also the words *beevers, bullock,
kine*, and *lamb*. As to wilder fauna, the *Plo* folk have terms for the
cormorant, crane, crocodile, locust, stag, stork, swan, vulture, and *whale*,
all of which are unknown to the *Min* people; and they have a smattering
of scientific vocables like *insect, reptile*, and *serpent*. The *Min* people
have a longer list of tame animals exclusive to them, viz. the *ass, camel*,

112

dromedary, hind, hog, hound, ram, and *swine;* and they know of wild fauna like the *boar, cricket, cuckoo, hyaena* (so spelt), *lark, owl, porcupine, turtle-dove,* and *viper.*

Conceivably of use in determining the geographical location of the *Plo* folk's territory are their exclusive names of flora: *crocus, fig-tree, fir,* and *gourd,* whereas the *Min* people's habitat might be identified by their peculiar vegetation, to wit the *cowslip, cypress, daffodil, daisy, eglantine, hawthorn, hazel, lily, maple, musk-rose, oat, pink, poplar, primrose, sweet-briar, thyme,* and *willow.* The horticultural interest of the *Plo* folk is indicated by their words *arbour, shrub, tendril, timber, twig,* and *under-growth,* all of them unknown to the *Min* people, who on the other hand are concerned with *buds, canker, haycocks, hedgerows, mildew, saplings, sprouts, stacks, stubble,* and *vermin.*

Novel and important anthropological conclusions may stem from the peculiar anatomical vocabularies of the populations under investigation. Concerning the anatomy of the *Plo* folk, we know that they were possessed of *bowels, knees, legs, livers, nostrils, palates, skins, throats,* and *waists,* none of which is attested for the *Min* people, who, however, had the monopoly of *brains,* and were further characterized by *chins, complexions, eyesight, fingers, fists, foreheads, navels, spleens, toes,* and *wrists*—all of which, to borrow a formulaic expression beloved of Professor Page, the *Plo* folk *must have* lacked, if we may rely on the type of *argumentum ex silentio* so long in vogue among the anatomizers of Homer. As to parts of animals, the *Plo* vocabulary distinguished *mane, offal,* and the elephant's *trunk,* while the *Min* people had words for *fin, quill, talon,* and *teat.* The *Plo* folk apparently suffered from *asthmas, colics, dropsies, pests, plagues, scurf,* and *ulcers,* but they alone had the word *remedy.* The only affliction distinctive of the *Min* people seems to have been a tendency to *sneeze.*

In dress and armour, and in military and nautical terminology, exa-mination of the distinctive *Plo* and *Min* vocabularies gives some support to the theory that the *Plo* and *Min* cultures differ in their archaeological contexts. The *Plo* folk are decidedly more maritime in their activities, to judge by the words *anchor, bulwark, larboard, mast, oar, beach, fathom, ferry, hull, prow, skiff, maritime, seamen, veer, plunge, swim,* and *drown,* all of which are unknown to the *Min* people, whose exclusive nautical vocabulary is apparently confined to the vocable *haven.*

For civilian attire the *Min* people appear richer in terms, with *bonnet, scarf, frock, gown, tasselled, embroidery, sock, shoon, boots,* and *sandals;* one notes also their *wardrobe,* clearly a necessary article of furniture for their numerous habiliments. Exclusive to the *Plo* folk are only the words *hood* and *skirt*. In military matters the *Plo* folk alone have such grandiose conceptions as a *rampart*, a *portcullis*, and a *stronghold*, while the *Min* people content themselves with a modest *fort*. That proceeding which in the *Min* dialect is called a *tourney* is in the *Plo* speech a *tournament*; and the *Plo* folk go in for *armour, panoply, trappings, tents, pavilions, standards, gonfalons*, and *pennons*, all of which are unknown to the *Min* people. Nevertheless the *Min* people enjoy exclusive use of some important military items, notably *bridle* and *spur*, gauntlet, *habergeon, cuirass, axe*, and *mace*. They alone have *captains, colonels*, and *officers*, and *salute* them; their *soldiery* includes *archers* and *cuirassiers*; they alone know such terms as *stratagem, harass, straggle, buffet, coward*, and *waver*. Perhaps one must think of the *Min* people as specializing in mounted archers with Parthian tactics. What the *Plo* folk term a *corpse*, the *Min* dialect more poetically pronounces as *corse*; oddly enough, their adjective *gory* is not applied to it. The developed terminology of warfare among the *Plo* folk has a different, more pedestrian, emphasis, exemplified by such words as *infantry, parade, encamp, regiment, battalion, vanguard, phalanx, breastplate, javelin, lance, targe, nitrous powder, clarion, drum, ambush, breach, fray, havoc, massacre, halt, disband, refuge, escape, mutiny, rebellious, volley, wage, war, onset, struggle, retreat*, and *surrender*. Since, on Professor Page's principles of argument, the two peoples "must have" lived in reciprocally isolated regions, it is a matter of sheer speculation to conjecture which side would win in the unlikely event of a hostile encounter. It is, indeed, improbable that either would win, since the *Plo* hoplites and fleet could hardly overtake the *Min* mounted archers, while the *Min* horsemen could not reduce the *maritime stronghold* of the *Plo* power.

Differences in social and political structure of the *Plo* and *Min* communities are indicated by their peculiar words expressing kinship, personal relations, professional status, and the like. For example, *Plo* alone has the word *clan*, and its characteristic words for family relationships are rather general terms, viz. *ancestor, progenitor, grandchild*, and *spouse*. Where the *Plo* folk know only the notion of *spouse*, the *Min* people have words for *bride* and *bridegroom*, and also *concubine, maiden, babe*, and *bastard*, suggesting that their culture was more evolved and discriminating. Of course, *brains* were a *Min* monopoly.

Again, in matters of rank and social position, *Plo* offers *adherent, attendant, advocate, comforter, associate, colleague, substitute, subordinate,*

114

disciple, vicegerent, umpire, burgher, inhabitant, inmate, stranger, merchant, peasant, seaman, historian, theologian, idiot, Seneschal, Sultan, Patriarch, Archangel, and *Apostate,* none of which is found in *Min.* Showing once more their superior evolution and discrimination, the *Min* people possess exclusively such terms of rank as *baron, captain, Earl, lady, magistrate, Marchioness, master, officer, President, proconsul, Senator, Tetrarch, Viscount;* such words descriptive of status as *neighbour, passenger, pensioner, swain, underling,* and *villager;* a diversity of occupational names like *barber, carpenter, carrier, chauntress, doctor, hedger, lackey,* and *shepherdess;* not to mention *genius, heretic, necromancer, wizard, ghost, spectre, hag, hermit, boy, lad, miser, murtherer, robber, politician, prelate, wrestler, wassailer, presbyter,* and *poet.*

Pursuing the archaeological indications, we note that the *Plo* folk alone have *brick, tiles, stairs, timber, boards, planks,* and *ceilings.* The *Min* people, on the other hand, exclusively possess words for *column* and *chimney, chamber, rafters,* and *eaves.* Their environment seems in some ways to have been more evolved from a town-planning point of view, their *hamlets* having an *inn,* a *mill,* and a *terrace,* on which perhaps were erected the *scaffolds* known to the *Min* dialect. Peculiar to the *Plo* community is a *thoroughfare* with a *pavement.* The actual word *furniture* is exclusive to the *Plo* folk, but the only furnishing item characteristic of them is the *divan;* whereas the more evolved *Min* people have such appurtenances as a *sideboard,* a *wardrobe, statues,* a *cradle,* a *bolster,* and even a *bier,* doubtless in connexion with the *funeral,* a peculiar *Min* ceremony.

About their gardens and farms the *Plo* folk have such features as an *arbour,* a *dairy, hive, kennel, pond,* and *wicket,* while they alone refer to *gardening* and *manuring.* Exclusive to the *Min* people are the terms *barndoor, carriage, cart, flail, haycock, manger, roost, stable, stack,* and *wicker.* While the *Plo* folk speak characteristically of *cash,* the *Min* people use the terms *coin* and *money,* doubtless kept in their *coffers, casket,* or *chest.*

When it comes to the important activities of eating and drinking, the *Plo* folk are poorly off, with merely an *egg, dregs,* some *kernels,* and *offal,* that they can call their own; while the *Min* people dispose not only of *ale* but of *wines* in the plural, which they drink to the *lees,* and they have such peculiar enjoyments as *julep, junkets, opium, pastry,* and *syrups,* with *dishes* wherein to accommodate them. *Trade* is a term unknown to the *Plo* folk, but it was doubtless partly by *trade* that the *Min* people obtained their richer equipment of what they call *utensils,* and the miscellaneous artefacts peculiar to them, such as the *axe, comb, lantern, razor, spit, sponge, tub, studs*, *tapers*, *thread*, *silk*, *wool*, *hooks*, and *cords*. With their greater abundance the *Min* people could afford a *holiday* now and then, taking along what they term their *luggage*. Their possession of *carts* and *carriages* bears out the notion, prompted by the study of their military equipment, that the *Min* people made considerable use of horses. Among what *Plo* folk call *implements* the peculiar one specified is the *whip*. Did this backward community employ that *implement* only on the *cattle* that they alone possessed, or also on their wives and children? It is typical of the superior discrimination and evolution of *Min* culture that their speech has the terms *microscope* and *telescope*, where the *Plo* folk talk clumsily about a *glazed optic tube*.

One could investigate the different musical and kindred activities of the two cultures, the *Plo* folk employing such terms as *cadence*, *chord*, *clarion*, *drum*, *dulcimer*, *lyre*, *recorder*, doubtless for their peculiar *parades*, *processions*, and *orgies*. The *Min* people have *cymbals* and *rebecks* as their characteristic instruments, and they perform *anthems*, *odes*, *jigs*, and *madrigals*, in the course of their *revelry* and *antics*. Again, there are fields to explore in connexion with their varying measurements of time and space. Will Professor Page ascribe to mere chance the fact that the *Min* people lack the word *autumn*, which the *Plo* folk have? The *Plo* dialect uses the terms *hourly*, *monthly*, and *yearly*, where *Min* has just *weekly*. *Min* has *today*, but not *yesterday*, a peculiarity of *Plo*, which, however, eschews *Min*'s term of *yore*. Why does *Min* call *sunrise* that time of day which *Plo* calls *dawning*, and *azurn* (twice) that colour which *Plo* thrice terms *azure*?

Enough has now been stated to prove, on the accepted principles of the Homeric *Chorizontes*, how untenable is the naïve traditionalist view that one and the same John Milton was author alike of *Paradise Lost* and of the lesser English poems that have been for centuries uncritically printed under his name. A noble series of articles and books could easily be produced by enterprising scholars who should apply the Pagean principles to the analysis of individual Miltonic poems that superficially appear to be unitary productions. Many words are not found in the second half of *Paradise Lost* that occur in the first half. And who can doubt that, as with the *Odyssey*, the end of *Samson Agonistes* was written later than the rest of it? If, at some remote future period, the discerptors of Milton should exhaust the resources of post-Wolfian Homeric theorizing, they may still find a fresh ruse or two in the tactical manuals of the Baconian assailants of Shakespeare, an author whom Professor Page, with an astonishing lapse into naïve traditionalism, admits (p. 160) to be the only superior of the poet of the *Odyssey*. Indeed, might not some diligent adherent of the Higher Statistical Criticism demonstrate from the occurrence and non-occurrence of words that the Page who penned the first half of *The Homeric Odyssey* was a different person, dwelling in a different region, from the Deutero-Page who concocted the second half of the volume, after having turned over many new leaves in another lexicon?

Now it may be that some robust sceptic has not been wholly convinced by the foregoing contentions, and would rather entertain the possibility that the application to Milton of Professor Page's principles of separatist criticism has tended somewhat in the direction of reducing those principles to absurdity. But let this sceptic observe that any such *reductio ad absurdum* applies primarily to the merely numerical aspects of the occurrence and absence of single words. Professor Page's theory, that the *Odyssey* was composed (later than the *Iliad*) and transmitted in a separate linguistic region, is, to a very small extent, based also on a few qualitative considerations about single words, and on study of phrases of two or more words. For instance, he asks (p. 164, n. 24) how we may account for the fact that "the same thing may be denoted in the *Iliad* by one word, in the *Odyssey* by another, e.g. αἰδοῖα (*Il.*) = μήδεα (*Od.*)." Looking more closely at this problem posed by Professor Page, we find that αἰδοῖα occurs only once in the *Iliad*, at xiii. 568, while μήδεα occurs four times in the *Odyssey*. Metrical convenience may well have been the motive for the choice of one synonym rather than the other.

Professor Page writes also (ibid.) of "the Odyssean use of ἄρτος (xvii. 343, xviii. 120) for σῖτος." In both passages ἄρτος seems to mean "a cake or loaf of wheat-bread" (so Liddell & Scott, rev. Jones–McKenzie). The *Odyssey* uses σῖτος very freely, some sixty-six times according to Cunliffe, in various senses, including that of "bread," but without the specific sense of "loaf" that ἄρτος has. The other examples given by Professor Page are the Odyssean use of κυνηγέτης (once, ix. 120) for the *Iliad*'s θηρητήρ, and of ὑπόδημα (twice, xv. 369, xviii. 361) for πέδιλον. Again it might be thought that metrical convenience was the determining factor, and it is hard to see why Professor Page should find an explanation in the alleged lateness of the *Odyssey* relative to the *Iliad*. The lateness may be relatively slight, and within the lifetime of a single author. Homer might well, like W. B. Yeats, have gone on till his dying day altering his poems, making additions or subtractions or verbal changes, small or large, for different audiences.

Professor Page touches also (p. 164, n. 24) on the doctrine that the

117

same word may denote different things in the *Iliad* and the *Odyssey*, giving as examples δνοπαλίζω at *Il*. iv. 472 and *Od*. xiv. 512, where the difference in shades of meaning seems slight, and ἀπριάτην, which is alleged to be adjectival at *Il*. i. 99 and adverbial at *Od*. xiv. 317. It can be adverbial at both places. But even if the *Iliad* example be truly adjectival, one recalls that the adverbial use developed from the feminine accusative of the adjective, and the process may still have been going on in Homer's lifetime, and have been slightly more advanced when he came to write the *Odyssey*. Alternatively, he may have taken over the phrases as they stood in his orally traditional sources for the different passages. Like Mr. Colin Hardie, "I don't mind accusing my Homer of inconsistent uses of the same word," whether through misunderstandings of old words and phrases, or by new extensions of meaning.[1]

Illustrations of the incidence of mere chance in Milton's use of single words do not affect quite directly Professor Page's arguments about the incidence of Homeric formulae, because the Miltonic language is much less formulaic, for various historical reasons, chiefly that his literary ancestry was predominantly *livresque*; and, so far as Milton does repeat phrases of two or more words, there appears to be no comprehensive study of them from which one can make up statistics as from a concordance. Indirectly, however, granted that there was a common stock of formulaic word-groups, as there was of single words, available to a single author of the *Iliad* and *Odyssey*, the play of mere chance in the occurrence of single words goes a long way to prove a similar play of chance in the occurrence or absence of formulae.

Moreover, Homeric Unitarians might use an argument which Mr˙ Colin Hardie kindly allows me to quote from a letter of his: "It is quite easy to put forward a hypothesis to account for new formulae in the *Odyssey* without supposing a new author: e.g. Homer could have visited another school of ἀοιδοί, new to him, and heard the deep-sea tales of the far west and Odysseus' wanderings there, and have seen the possibilities of another long poem incorporating them." My colleague Professor Kenneth Dover emphasizes also that we should not under-estimate the fertility of a poet of Homer's calibre in himself inventing new formulae for different parts of his compositions. It is natural for an author, on attaining some note, to travel, and to pick up new ideas and new phrases. Even politicians and dons undergo a similar process.

---

[1] See his article, "In Defence of Homer," *Greece and Rome,* Second Series, iii (1956), 123.

Professor Page, early in his discussion of the vocabulary of the *Odyssey*, remarks (p. 149) that "the topic requires, and would amply repay, a full investigation." Pending such a full investigation, desultory lists and notes such as his ought not to be pressed into service to support so far-reaching a theory as the Regius Professor of Greek at Cambridge has propounded. Thanks no doubt largely to Professor Page's brilliant reputation for his contributions in other fields, the theory appears to be becoming a wide-spread dogma, having won substantial acceptance from good scholars like Professors P. Chantraine and J. A. Davison.

Many students of Homeric, and other Greek, vocabulary have apparently not yet come sufficiently to grips with some of the fundamental problems of statistical analysis. Properly handled, it is capable of yielding useful results where the mass of material is large enough, as in the evolution of Platonic vocabulary studied by such scholars as Lewis Campbell and H. von Arnim, with a view to the relative dating of dialogues. I am indebted to Mr. Bernard Babington Smith for knowledge of G. Udny Yule's essay, *The Statistical Study of Literary Vocabulary* (Cambridge University Press, 1944), which is worth the attention of classical students.

Udny Yule's original interest lay in the problem of ascription of the *De imitatione Christi*, for which he studied the vocabularies used by Thomas à Kempis and by Jean Gerson. *Compendi causa* I cite some figures from Yule's subsidiary analysis of four essays by Macaulay, written in the years 1825, 1831, and 1842, respectively on Milton, Hampden, Bacon, and Frederick the Great. Of 3,543 nouns listed in the samples studied by Yule only 402 occurred in all four essays over this period of 17 years—just over 11 per cent.; 1,898 (53·6 per cent.) occurred in only some one of the four essays; 471 occurred in three out of the four; and 772 in two out of the four.

From the same table (Yule, op. cit., p. 149, Table 7.1) one notes that, in samples studied from four different works of John Bunyan (dated over the years 1678 to 1684), out of 2,244 nouns listed only 259 (less than 12 per cent.) occur in all four of the samples examined, while 1,250 (56 per cent.) are found in only one of the four works. These rigorous numerical computations are objective, and on a different basis from the mainly subjective arguments of Monsignor Ronald Knox in his *Essays* in *Satire* (Sheed & Ward, London, repr. 1936), whereby he purported to demonstrate that the second part of *The Pilgrim's Progress* was written not by John Bunyan but by some Anglican lady who was only awaiting the King's official return to Romanism to proclaim her own Popery.

Emeritus Professor H. J. Rose reminds me that P. Groeneboem, in his edition of Aeschylus' *Prometheus* (Groningen, 1928, p. 18), noted a dissertation of Fr. Niedzballa, *De copia verborum et elocutione Promethei Vincti q.f. Aeschylei* (Breslau, 1913), where, by a list of 640 words (including proper names) found in the *P.V.* and not elsewhere in Aeschylus, the thesis-writer sought to prove the spuriousness of the *P.V.* Groeneboem states that he set a pupil of his own to list the words in the *Persai* not found elsewhere in plays ascribed to Aeschylus, and he found 596 (not counting proper names). Perhaps Professor Page will now enter the lists to maintain that neither the *Prometheus* nor the *Persai* was written by Aeschylus, but that both were stitched together by committees of local amateur dramatic societies in linguistically isolated regions of Hellas.

From *Edinburgh in the Age of Walter Scott*

Chapter 7, in the *Centres of Civilization* Series of the University of
Oklahoma Press, © 1965.

CASTES AND FASHIONS

THOUGH IN SCOTT'S TIME the classes of Edinburgh society mingled as a rule
in a friendly and familiar way, still there was marked class consciousness
at all levels. In *The Autobiography of a Working Man*, Somerville complains
that "The masons were intolerable tyrants to their labourers." In contrast
Lord Provost Creech laments the high wages and indiscipline of journey-
men in the 1790's: "Many of them riot on Sunday, are idle all Monday,
and can afford to do this on five days labour." Maidservants, with three or
four pounds of wages a year, "dress as fine as their mistresses."

At the top of the social tree were, of course, the Scots peers and their
ladies. When George IV came in August, 1822, and held a levee at Holyrood, 63 peers paraded, followed by 77 baronets, and some 2,000 untitled
gentlemen. Some of the Highland chiefs appeared with "tails" of men at
arms in tartan kilts; and Sir Walter Scott, who stage-managed the visit,
wore a kilt himself, of Campbell tartan for some female ancestress, and
persuaded George IV to appear, twice, in a kilt of Stewart tartan. The
portly monarch wore silk tights beneath it. The even portlier Lord Mayor
of London wore a kilt too. At the peers' ball only reels and strathspeys and
other national dances were performed; but the Caledonian Hunt added
waltzes to theirs. A separate levee was held for ministers and elders of the
kirk. At the annual levees of the King's High Commissioner to the General
Assembly, a Scots peer, it was more or less socially obligatory for heads
of landowning families, even if not Presbyterian, to show a leg, along with
the rural ministers and elders, and the judges and advocates. The top-
ranking lords and lairds might be members of the Royal Company of
Archers, with its handsome uniform, and the not quite-so-top men might
be found in the corps of High Constables of Holyrood, founded in 1787.
The parliamentary elections for the sixteen Scots representative peers were
great social occasions, with much petticoat government in the background,

dowagers intriguing for votes, where there were, as Lord Kinnaird put it, "more piglets than teats." The elected sixteen would give dinners or balls, one of which James Boswell describes. Peers were to be seen about the town wearing the broad ribbons and stars of orders they might possess, and they addressed one another as "Your Lordship" or "My Lord," until long after Scott's day. There were thousands of non-titled Scots related to these top persons, and very well aware of the cousinship, however remote: so that foreigners remarked a certain aristocratic tone in the behaviour of professional and commercial men who in other countries would not have been so highly regarded socially.

The judges were accorded suitable respect, with a grain of salt, even by themselves. Lord President Forbes proposed a toast: "Here's to such of the judges as don't deserve the gallows." Lord Kames, on leaving the bench, said, "Fare ye weel, ye bitches." And a certain frivolity kept intruding even from the bench. In sentencing to death one Matthew Hay, with whom he had played chess, Kames remarked: "That's checkmate to you, Mattha!" Presiding at the trial of Gerard, one of the Friends of the People, when the reformer observed that Jesus Christ had been a reformer too, Braxfield retorted: "Muckle he made o' that. He was hangit." Squabbles for precedence among officeholders broke out during a great fire near the Law Courts in 1824. Cockburn says it was "rather sternly discussed on the street whether the Lord Provost could order the Justice-Clerk to prison, or the Justice the Provost, and whether George Cranstoun, the Dean of the Faculty, was bound to work at an engine, when commanded by John Hope, the Solicitor-General, to do so, or *vice versa*."

The Advocates were the most characteristic body of Edinburgh society, with plenty of time on their hands. Soon after Scott's time there were no fewer than 462 members of the Faculty, of whom 92 were authors. Not many more than a dozen made good incomes from practice; the rest had inherited money or married it. There were also a good many army officers hanging about Edinburgh, either in the castle garrison, which numbered about 2,000 at maximum, or retired on half-pay. Those who had served in India looked down on the rest. By London standards, Edinburgh had no dandies; but these gentlemen of leisure ran the organized amusements, such as horse-racing on Leith sands; curling, if the winter brought enough cold for ice; golfing, in red coats, at Bruntsfield or Leith; and cockfighting. Duels were rare. Phrenology had a brief vogue.

Writers to the Signet and other lawyers had to keep office-hours, as did the merchants and shopkeepers. Early seekers of news would gather at the Cross at 7.00 a.m., and shops would open after breakfast at 8.00. Merchants did business in the open air, rather than at their Exchange. At 11.30 the bells of St Giles would play tunes, and there would be a general exodus to the innumerable taverns for the first alcoholic drink of the day, apart from the small ale taken with the breakfast porridge. Shops shut from 12.00 until 2.00 for dinner, which in most homes was vegetable broth with oatcakes and cheese, sometimes meat on Sundays, and often fish. Vegetables were retailed by a sorority of gin-drinking old women round the Cross. A bell at 8.00 p.m. was the signal for shutting shops for the day, and tradesmen normally then spent an hour or two in a tavern. The innumerable clubs, whether for music or debate or literature or plain drinking, normally met in taverns (pubs). A roll of drums at 10.00 was the signal for shutting the taverns, and for emptying excreta from the windows: so that the home-going reveler often had to cry in alarm, "Haud your hand!"

The gentry dined at two or three o'clock around 1770, but about five or six o'clock later on. Formal dinners were boring by reason of the obligation for every diner to toast every other diner individually, and to propose sentiments, such as "Mair freends and less need o' them," or "Delicate pleasures to susceptible minds." Suppers were much preferred, as cheaper, shorter, less ceremonious, and more poetical. Ladies held tea parties, between four and six, at one time with gentlemen present; the silver spoons were each numbered, to avoid confusion on refilling; and the etiquette was to leave the spoon in the cup, not in the saucer, when one wished no further supply. Cards often followed the tea. A coffeehouse had been opened in 1675, but tea was much more relished, often laced with whisky, which only cost 10d. a quart. Rum and sugar had come in from the 1680's. With sugar and lemons and hot water, fortified by rum, whisky, or brandy, a convivial group would brew a punch, and ladle it round the glasses. Scots silverwork had long been fine, and at this time became more abundant. The practice of destroying a glass after drinking a toast gradually went out.

In ordinary families supper was again porridge, and the appurtenances of the table were modest, usually just wooden bowls and cups and horn spoons. But the gentry enjoyed standards in plate, porcelain, foods, and wines as high as most in Europe. A Scots partiality was for five-year-old mutton and old claret, David Hume's favourite repast. John Home wrote an epigram on the shift from French claret to Portuguese port, occasioned by English political alliances:

Firm and erect the Caledonian stood;
old was his mutton, and his claret good.
"Let him drink port!" the Saxon statesman cried.
He drank the poison, and his spirit died.

The judge Lord Newton never did business without imbibing six pints of claret, and could keep as clear a head as need be. Jeffrey, in his country house at Craigcrook, held parties where dinner, at five, was preceded by a contest in long jumping, and thirty-two sorts of wine were on hand. He preferred champagne, which came in after 1815.

Edinburgh was fortunate in supplies of fresh seafish, and lobsters, oysters, and mussels. The fishermen's womenfolk were a remarkable breed. They could carry a hundredweight of wet fish many miles up country. Three of them were recorded as walking from Dunbar to Edinburgh, twenty-seven miles, each with a two-hundred-pound load. If the boats came in late, the Inveresk women would run the five miles to Edinburgh inside forty-five minutes, in relays, each carrying the basket one hundred yards, to get the fish to market in time for dinner. These women played at golf and football, and many of them were popular dancers. Fashionable folk from the New Town liked to spend an evening in a cellar night club of the Old Town, with oysters and porter, a strong type of beer, seeing the oyster-women dance. A raffish tone had been current even before the Regency. It was fashionable for ladies to be pretty free-spoken, and to use oaths. Hume remarks that in French *salons* there was "Scarce a double Entendre to be heard; scarce a free Joke." He solemnly defends "bawdy" to the Lord Advocate, writing: "I know not a more agreeable subject both for books and conversation, if executed with decency and ingenuity."

Edinburgh people were also great scandalmongers. Lord Kames picked up gossip every day from one "Sinkum the Cawdie," on his way to Court. This was a member of the fraternity of caddies, who hung about the Cross, to run errands. They knew everybody and everything, and helped to prevent crime accordingly. If one were ever dishonest, the fraternity made good his employer's loss.

There seems, indeed, to have been remarkably little crime in Edinburgh before the 1790's; but, as Creech remarked, "As opulence increases, virtue subsides." In 1805 an unarmed police was instituted. Previously, there had been a city guard of veteran soldiers, with Lochaber axes, a combination of spear, axe, and hook. The most sensational criminality was that of Burke and Hare, who in the 1820's murdered people to sell their corpses to anatomists. Scott reported in 1812 the discovery of "a formal association among nearly fifty apprentices aged from twelve to twenty to scour the streets and knock down and rob all whom they found in their way." They had been meeting for months, and keeping regular minutes; and executed their grand design on the last night of the year, hogmanay. But this specimen of concerted juvenile delinquency seems to be unique. On the other hand, mob violence broke out now and again, for instance, in 1779, in protest against the toleration of Roman Catholicism, when the historian Robertson's house was burned down; and in 1832, for the carrying of the Reform Bill, when a mob of thousands smashed the windows of Tories who would not light up to celebrate. The slogan was, "Up with Reform light! Down with Tory darkness!" Mudie comments on the diligence of artisans in attending evening classes, which he found made them more formidable as a mob when they chose to riot. This was part of the sharpening class conflict towards the end of Scott's life.

The licensed beggars were a privileged small group, with their blue gowns, and their purses, annually replenished by as many pence as the reigning king had years. There was a regulation sum to give them, and gentlemen who did not have it exact were not ashamed to ask change amounting to one-sixth of a penny. The afflux of unlicensed beggars from the countryside was resisted; but after 1825, when there was a general financial crisis, Edinburgh became full of unemployed building workers, and schemes of emergency poor relief had to be undertaken, as in 1795 and 1816. A distinct caste, too, were the sedan-chair carriers, mainly Gaelic-speakers; but the move to the New Town reduced them to vanishing point. Coal porters and water carriers were distinctive trades, requiring soundness of heart to carry loads up and down the tall common stairs of the tenements.

For wage earners in such industries as existed the hours of labour were long at bad times. Somerville worked in a saw pit from 6.00 a.m. to 7.00 p.m., living on porridge morning and night, and broth for dinner, with meat never and bread seldom. He drank *soor dook*, a raw kind of buttermilk; and spent his money on books and writing materials; he was one of an exceptionally able and aspiring minority among the underprivileged, but he observes that most Scottish soldiers could write and keep accounts, whereas few could do so in English or Irish regiments. The Shorter Catechism given by Presbyterians to their children often had the multiplication tables printed on the back, to rear a generation both godly and calculating.

Somerville describes his dress in 1831 as thick shoes, corduroy trousers, a fustian coat, and a blue bonnet. The upper ranks wore tail coats and top hats by then, having discarded breeches, cloaks, and three-cornered hats. At home at leisure they sat around in caps and nightgowns. Scott in his country house, at Abbotsford, dressed, says Cockburn, like a smuggler or a poacher. "His simplicity and naturalness after all his fame are absolutely incredible." In general foreigners seem to have been struck by the naturalness of Scottish behaviour. Buzonnière notes that the Scots "have too much imagination to preserve the cold dignity of the English gentlemen." Though Oliver Goldsmith, in 1753, had found the Scots behaving at dances with "a formality approaching to despondence," Lockhart in the 1820's comments on Scots dancers "glorying in muscular agitation and alertness." The English Captain Topham found that "The air of mirth and vivacity, that quick penetrating look, that spirit of gaiety which distinguished the French, is equally visible in the Scotch." A London lady, Mrs Elizabeth Montagu, notes that the Scots "live in ye french way, *des petits soupers fins*, & they have ye easy address of the french." Cobbett, writing from Edinburgh, states: ". . . better manners never were exhibited in this world than by my audiences here," and "Every man that I have met with at Edinburgh has been as kind to me as if he were my brother." Lockhart, an Anglicanized snob of the type that became commoner after Scott's time, writes: "People visit each other in Edinburgh with all the appearance of cordial familiarity, who, if they lived in London, would imagine their differences of rank to form an impassable barrier against such intercourse."

It was precisely the habit of kindly intercourse among different income groups and occupational types that promoted the development of diverse talent in Edinburgh. William Smellie, editor of the first *Encyclopaedia Britannica*, quoted a comment of Mr Amyat, the King's chemist, who had resided in Edinburgh a year or two: "Here I stand at what is called the *Cross of Edinburgh*, and can, in a few minutes, take fifty men of genius and learning by the hand. . . . In Edinburgh, the access of men of parts is not only easy, but their conversation and the communication of their knowledge are at once imparted to intelligent strangers with the utmost liberality. The philosophers of Scotland have no nostrums. They tell what they know, and deliver their sentiments without disguise or reserve." Mudie remarks that the people of "the modern Athens" had "gusto, and grace, and gravity." It must have been a most exciting city to live in, with Walter Scott and so many more as fellow citizens.

From *St Andrews: Town and Gown, Royal and Ancient*

Chapter 12. Cassel, London, 1969. Written in his typically flippant.
racy, humorous manner.

THE GROWING UNIVERSITY

OF THE TRIO—Religion, Golf, and Learning—the third was a poor third
till quite late in the nineteenth century, at any rate as regards secular
learning. Religion, or at least theology, was dominant, even over golf.
When Sir Walter Scott first came to St Andrews, in 1793, and cut runes
into the turf by the castle gateway to spell out the name of the lady who
had rejected his addresses, Williamina Stuart Belshes, a third of the undergraduates were students of Divinity, and most of the professors were also
Ministers of the Church of Scotland as by law established. There were
forty-eight students in St Mary's, a hundred in the United College. Almost
till Queen Victoria's death the divinity students dominated the social
activities of the little university. After all, they pursued their studies for
more years than those reading for the degree in arts. It was only the
"divines" who reached an age at which whiskers and beards could luxuri-
ate, and whose muscular development became capable of disciplining the
entire local police force by throwing him into the harbour at the start of
the Martinmas Term in autumn.

Typical, in his interests, of the nineteenth century is Thomas Jackson,
born in St Andrews in 1797. He held chairs of divinity at St Mary's and
Glasgow from 1836 to 1874, and then returned to St Andrews to write his
great work, designed to settle all the controversies of the centuries and
bring discordant Scots into unanimity. He had one of the big houses on
the south side of South Street, with its "lang rigg," at the foot of which
was an elegant garden-room, with a table and a chair. Hither daily the
septuagenarian resorted, garbed in his ecclesiastical frock-coat, took off
his shiny top hat, and grasped a quill pen to set down his great thoughts
on the virgin white folio quire daily laid out on the table. After several
hours he would tear it all up and go back to the house. After four years
they found him dead, aged eighty-one, and the garden-house yielded a

single written sheet with the sum of his wisdom: "Theology is everything, and everything is theology."

Professor Jackson is described as "a mystic of the highest order, and one of the kindliest of men." In this he was not so typical of the Andreapolitan religionists, many of whom could be quite worldly and waspish. For example, in the mid-Victorian "revival" promoted by the American evangelists Dwight L. Moody and Ira D. Sankey, when the rest of the Andreapolitans began confessing their sins in public, Principal Shairp of the United College went round confessing to various hearers the sins of his colleague John Tulloch, the Principal of St Mary's. Religious disputes were, of course, not all just about theology, but very often about Church government, and who would have what job, and what should be the architectural style of a church, or the mode of its worship. In considering the evolution of these activities it is perhaps most convenient to make the development of the university, small as it was, the core of the narrative. In recent decades, indeed, the university has become the economic and social core of the town.

The later eighteenth century saw the Church of Scotland dominated by the so-called Moderates. In contrast to the minority of "High-Flyers," the Moderates cultivated elegance and urbanity in deportment and utterance, and inclined to rationalism in the defence of Calvinist orthodoxy. Earlier in the century Archibald Campbell, a St Andrews professor, asserted that the Apostles had been "no enthusiasts." Of this breed was George Hill (1750-1819), son of a St Andrews Minister. He got the Greek chair at twenty-one, and became Principal of St Mary's in 1791. Not only did he dominate the General Assembly of the Church, but before long it was found that, of the thirteen members of the academic Senatus, six belonged to tne Hill family. Worshippers came to relish the 121st Psalm in its metrical version: "I to the Hills will lift mine eyes, From whence doth come mine aid." A cosy academic job of that period was the sale of St Leonard's College to Professor Robert Watson, for £200 and a £10 annual feu duty. He demolished the bonny bell-tower, and removed the roof of the chapel to make it a greenhouse. The shrubs did not thrive, but the professor did well by taking in aristocratic boarders into the old college buildings, now his private house. Maitland Anderson, sometime University Librarian, found in the margin of a book a comment by a student of this period: "Every kind of dissipation was carried on openly, and never checked by any professor."

The vandalism at St Leonard's College was paralleled at St Salvator's,

128

where the original Gothic roof had a rather flat arch, and there was an echo that made every sermon seem twice as long. After a report in 1773 by James Craig, planner of the New Town of Edinburgh, the professors had the roof cut away at the wallheads and dropped bodily into the church, wrecking the elaborate Gothic tomb of the pious founder. However, a spirit of improvement was stirring in the cultural climate, and reached even St Andrews, as manifested in the careers of Andrew Bell and Thomas Chalmers.

Andrew Bell was son of a local bailie and hairdresser, who experimented in type-founding with Alexander Wilson (1714-86), later Professor of Astronomy at Glasgow, where he designed types for the Foulis Press. At the age of eighteen, in 1781, the young Bell set out to the Witch Hill one morning to fight a duel with an English student: being short-sighted, he fired at the seconds instead of the antagonist. No harm was done; and Bell took to religion, ending up as a canon of Westminster Abbey, where he was buried in 1832, after endowing the Madras College, which put St Andrews on the Victorian educational map. Thomas Chalmers was born in 1780, along the coast at Anstruther; he came to college at the age of eleven, and was good at football and handball. His main bent was mathematical, but through family influence he became in 1803 Minister of Kilmany parish, about ten miles away, riding over to lecture as assistant to the Regius Professor of Mathematics, Nicolas Vilant. At the oral examination the two preceptors disagreed, and Chalmers delivered a long invective, which led to the ending of his assistantship. Nothing daunted, Chalmers ran a class of his own in the next session, with numerous students attending. He defied the Presbytery to stop him, maintaining that "after the satisfactory discharge of his parish duties a minister may enjoy five days in the week of uninterrupted leisure for the prosecution of any science in which his taste may dispose him to engage." Around the same time William Ferrie, Minister of Kilconquhar, held the chair of civil history for eighteen years (1808-26), and gave only two lectures. Chalmers had an illness in 1810, during which he experienced a religious conversion; his sermons began to attract crowds to Kilmany from far afield. In 1814 he was called to the Tron kirk in Glasgow, and began to campaign for the rescue of the poor folk in industrial cities. In 1823 St Andrews made him Professor of Moral Philosophy, where he lectured mainly on political economy; and in 1828 he removed to Edinburgh as Professor of Divinity, taking a leading part in the movement that led to the Disruption of the Church of Scotland in 1843, of which anon.

As rebuilt in 1754 St Salvator's had rooms for only some forty resident students, and most of them lived in the town, sometimes boarding with professors. As Chancellor (1765-88), the eighth Earl of Kinnoull encouraged gentlefolk to settle with their families for golf and education. So did his successor, Harry Dundas, first Viscount Melville (1788-1811), called "the uncrowned king of Scotland" for his Tory political management. His son Robert was also Chancellor (1814-51), and got the Government to give some money for rebuilding the decrepit quadrangle of St Salvator's. In 1828 Robert Reid, the King's Architect, erected a large Jacobean structure, providing only four classrooms, all too big. He also did some restoration and alteration at St Mary's and the University Library, more intelligently. Then the Whigs succeeded the Tories, and, as the Rev. Dr Grierson lamented in 1838, "the funds which had been honourably pledged for the completion of the United College were unceremoniously and unjustly given for the rebuilding of Marischal College, Aberdeen. Hence the United College of St Andrews stands a hideous compound of mean and gorgeous architecture, a proof of the faithlessness of public men. . . ." Many times since 1838 not only St Andrews but other universities could lament likewise.

In 1826 the Government appointed a Royal Commission, which reported in 1830; but nothing was done to implement its proposals till the Act of Parliament of 1858. In 1827 a new nine-subject Master of Arts degree curriculum was introduced: Humanity (Latin), Greek, Logic, Mathematics, Moral Philosophy, Natural Philosophy (Physics), Natural History, Chemistry, and Political Economy. But few graduated. For example, in 1845 three men graduated BA, three MA, one DD; but 106 bought the MD degree, which cost them twenty-five guineas a head, of which the Government took ten pounds for stamping the academic diploma. This paucity of graduates is the more curious that by 1845 the Madras College had about nine hundred pupils, and the town was still enjoying a boom as a "watering-place." There had been some nice Regency building, such as Pilmuir Links (1820), convenient for the golf-course and the sea. These elegant houses, writes Grierson, "are generally well filled during that season when invalids and hypochondriacs lave their limbs in the briny deep." In similar style he writes of the Lammas Fair in August, where farm-servants struck new bargains for the next year's feeing, and the visitor could enjoy "the unrestrained jollity of these unsophisticated children of the land." Since 1810, also, there had been baths on the clifftop west of the Castle, with hot water and showers for those who funked the

North Sea. An annual event was the carters' race, run by the Whiplickers' Society, from the Blue Stane, oldest sacral object in the burgh, now behind the railing of the Windsor and Station Hotel.

The religious and political movements that came to a head in the Disruption of 1843 had been simmering for generations. By a religious settlement annexed to the Treaty of Union of 1707, the Church of Scotland, as established on its Presbyterian basis in 1690, was guaranteed a monopoly for all time coming in Scotland. But in 1712 the recently created Parliament of the United Kingdom of Great Britain passed two Acts which were constitutionally beyond its powers as derived from the international treaty. A Toleration Act pretended to authorize Episcopalian worship in Scotland, and a Patronage Act gave local land-owners the power to present ministers to parish churches, whether the local congregation liked the presentee or not. After a series of General Assembly protests, a number of ministers seceded in 1733, and formed an Associate Presbytery. In 1747 these "Seceders" split into "Burghers," who accepted an oath imposed on new burgesses in certain burghs, to uphold "the true Protestant religion presently professed within this realm," and a rival body of "Anti-Burghers." The Burghers then split into "Auld Lichts," who upheld the Solemn League and Covenant of 1643, and "New Lichts," who thought it obsolete. By another split, there arose "Lifters," who allowed ministers to raise the bread and wine when consecrating them for a communion, and "Anti-Lifters," who prohibited such "papistical backslitherings." Gradually, however, the fissiparous sects began to coalesce again, and in 1820 arose the "United Secession" Church. In the 1820s a spirit of religious revival spread through much wider strata, and in 1824 the General Assembly of the Established Church adopted an overture to institute foreign missions. Famous among the missionaries was a St Andrews graduate of 1829, Alexander Duff, who went to India in 1830, being shipwrecked twice. His Bible, rescued from the waves, keeps company in the University Library with the Koran of Tippoo Sahib, and the Bible of Donald Cargill, the Covenanter, who was captured in 1681, in Charles II's "killing times." Another St Andrews alumnus, the dissolute Duke of Rothes, who had signed the two Covenants as a student, threatened Cargill with extraordinary torture and violent death, to which Cargill retorted, "Die what death I will, your eyes will not see it." The debauched duke died suddenly the night before Cargill was hanged. It was by a revival of interest in such Presbyterian martyrs as Cargill that people subscribed to erect in 1842 the obelisk at the west end of the Scores commemorating four of the sixteenth-century Protestants executed by the Papalists.

With the revived evangelical stirrings, more and more people began to rebel against the imposition of presentees on parishes by land-owners, many of whom were themselves Episcopalians or indifferent in matters of religion. A series of litigations arose in the 1830s, but the law courts invariably upheld the right of land-owners to intrude ministers of their own choice whatever a congregation might wish. Finally, in 1843, at the annual General Assembly, a massive minority of ministers and elders walked out, in protest against the refusal of the government and Parliament to remedy the grievance. In all, 451 out of about 1,200 ministers and a third of the communicants left the "Auld Kirk" to found the Free Church of Scotland. Thomas Chalmers used his mathematical ability to organize a sustentation fund, which soon was able to pay five hundred ministers £150 a year. Within four years the Free Kirk had seven hundred churches, and many schools, and its own colleges and overseas missions, including those founded by Alexander Duff. At the same time the ministers who had stayed in the Auld Kirk began to exert themselves to compete. Chalmers's chief opponent was his successor in the chair of moral philosophy, George Cook (1828-45), leader of the Moderates in the Assembly. A majority of the academics seem to have been Auld Kirkers, and they made life unhappy for the United College Principal, Sir David Brewster (1838-59), who was a Free Kirker. He was also hostile to the cosy jobbery of the Hill and Cook type, and always looked for the best man for any vacant chair. Himself a distinguished scientist, he wished the university to teach civil engineering and such social and economic studies as would be useful to bankers, merchants and manufacturers. Aided by the Presbytery of St Andrews, Brewster's colleagues tried to have him deposed; but they failed on a technicality, that he had not personally signed the deed of demission of office in the Established Church. He was glad to move off to be Principal of Edinburgh.

The Christian spirit of the 1840s is exemplified in the prayer of a Divinity student for a professor about whom he had his doubts: "Lord, have mercy on our Professor, for he is weak and ignorant. Strengthen his feeble hands, confirm his tottering knees, and grant that he may go out and in before us like the he-goat before the flock." Architects at least benefited from the rivalry of sects. In 1849 Dr Charles Roger noted the seating capacities of churches in St Andrews thus: the Toun Kirk, largely rebuilt in 1797, could seat 2,500; its overflow St Mary's (1839: now the

Victory Memorial Hall) held 630; the Martyrs' Free Kirk, opposite the College Kirk in North Street, built in 1844, held 870; and the United Presbyterian edifice at the east end of North Street (1826) could seat 450. An Independent Church in Market Street, enlarged in 1824, held 340; and the Baptist Church west of Madras College (1841) had 250. The small Episcopalian community, having long met in private houses, had built a smallish chapel in 1825 in North Street. They had 108 members in 1836, at which time there was only one Roman Catholic family, of Irish immigrants; not till 1884 could the Papalists afford a church, when they erected what Andrew Lang called "a corrugated place of worship," more vulgarly a "tin tabernacle," on the clifftop, just east of the Martyrs' Memorial. An old fisherman in 1930 told me how he had broken in, with others, and thrown the tall candles into the sea. In 1910 Reginald Fairlie was architect of the fine St James's Church on the same site. Today the Roman Catholic Society is the largest of the students' clubs; the oldest is the Theological Society, started in 1760. There was by 1849 seating accommodation for over 5,000 worshippers at a time, rather more than the total population of the burgh.

A tourist commented to his coachman, "There must be a great deal of religious zeal in this town: there are so many churches." To which the cynical Jehu replied, "It's no religious zeal ava. It's juist cursedness o' temper." Somewhat similarly I recall a chat with a chauffeur waiting on his mistress to emerge from a Buchmanite or "Oxford Group" meeting in the Town Hall in the 1930s. He thought it "juist a kind o' Salvation Airmy for the gentry." One effect of the Disruption in the university was that attendance at the College Kirk ceased to be compulsory. Till 1904 it was also the church of St Leonard's Parish, since the disuse of St Leonard's Chapel. From 1844 to 1904 there was intermittent wrangling and litigation between the St Leonard's congregation and the university, which ended with the removal of the St Leonard's people to a massive new Romanesque church in the opulent western suburban thoroughfare, Hepburn Gardens, put up at the cost of the feuars there, who grudged sorely the expense. One of them decided to get his money's worth by sending his wife to sit in the new church.

More building of the 1840s included the West Infant School (1844), in its day a new model Kindergarten for the Madras College; William Nixon's North building of St Salvator's quadrangle, in Jacobean style like Reid's East building; and the start of Mr Hope Scott's scheme to rival the New Town of Edinburgh, with Hope Street a straight terrace, Howard

Place a convex one, and Abbotsford Place a concave, all set round a park. It took half a century to complete. 1854 saw the substantial clubhouse erected for the Royal and Ancient, and the new Town Hall was built in 1861 in Scotch Baronial style. The railway came to St Andrews in 1854, and wealthy *rentiers* began to put up Scotch Baronial dream homes, like Kinburn, Edgecliffe, and Westerlea (now Wardlaw Hall). In 1859 a new Principal came to the United College, James David Forbes, an excellent geologist, son of the famous banker, Sir William Forbes, and of Walter Scott's first love, Williamina Stuart Belshes. A High Churchman, Forbes put stained glass into the College Kirk. He also sought to restore the residential system for students, and to make the undergraduate body truly representative by attracting boys from the old peerage families. In this he was aided by the chancellor, the eighth Duke of Argyll (1851-1900), who sent his son, who later married a daughter of Queen Victoria. A Marquis of Breadalbane and an Earl of Aberdeen were other alumni of this time; but the best known today was a scholar and writer, Andrew Lang.

Andrew Lang, a Borderer related to Walter Scott, came to St Andrews from the Edinburgh Academy in 1861, aged seventeen, his uncle, W. Y. Sellar, being Professor of Greek. He stayed in the College Hall, newly set up by Principal Forbes in a rented house on the site of St Leonard's College. He remembered it as:

> . . . something between an Oxford Hall and a Master's House at a public school, rather more like the latter than the former. We were more free than school-boys, not as free as undergraduates. There were about a dozen of us at first, either from the English public schools, or the Edinburgh Academy. Fate, and certain views of the authorities about the impropriety of studying human nature in St Andrews after dark, thinned our numbers very early in the first session.

The last Marquis of Breadalbane recalled:

> The two rules the students of the Hall most objected to were, that they were not to enter the billiard-rooms of any of the hotels in St Andrews, nor were they to accept an invitation to dinner or a party except on Friday and Saturday nights. Another bitter complaint was that the gas supplied was so meagre that it only made darkness visible.

In spite of all, the Hall throve enough for Forbes to have a new one specially built in 1868, which, however, failed in 1874. In 1877 the valuable site was sold to St Leonard's School for Girls, a new venture that has since acquired great renown. Already in 1836 the New Statistical Account had told of two boarding-houses for young ladies, in which "all the usual branches of education that are required for females in the higher ranks of life may be attained."

The most popular teacher in Lang's time was J. F. Ferrier, Professor of Moral Philosophy. Lang writes:

> There was I know not what of dignity, of humour, and of wisdom in his face; there was an air of the student, the vanquisher of difficulties, the discoverer of hidden knowledge, in him, that I have seen in no other. His method at that time was to lecture on the History of Philosophy, and his manner was so persuasive that one believed firmly in the tenets of each school he described, till he advanced those of the next! Thus the whole historical evolution of thought went on in the mind of each of his listeners.

Another student remembered Ferrier's series of variegated waistcoats, and his habit of arriving late and leaving early; and his ability to give students more to think about in fifteen minutes than any other teacher could give in an hour. Mrs Ferrier was less impressed, being a daughter of "Christopher North," of *Noctes Ambrosianae* fame. Of her husband's philosophy she said: "It makes you feel as if you were sitting upon a cloud with nothing on, a lucifer match in your hand, but with no possible way to strike it!" Her brother-in-law, the poet W. E. Aytoun, spent a week with them and returned to Edinburgh asserting that Hell was "a quiet and friendly place to live in compared with St Andrews."

Forbes was succeeded as Principal by John Campbell Shairp (1868-85), who objected to innovations lately made in the College Kirk, such as kneeling at prayer and standing at praise. He desired the students to wear blue bonnets with red tassels, instead of square mortar-boards, and wrote: "Anglicized Scotchmen are generally poor creatures, and an Anglicized Scotland will be a contemptible country." Shairp founded the Cottage Hospital, in memory of his mother-in-law, Lady William Douglas of Dunino (1864). It could not have pleased him that the historian J. A. Froude, elected Rector by the students, said of them in 1869, "These youths are exactly like Oxford undergraduates." By the Act of 1858 the undergraduates were allowed again to elect an extrinsic Rector, and the post has been filled by some most distinguished personalities. The longest rectorial address so far is that of J. S. Mill in 1867, 140 minutes. The judge Lord Neaves was Rector in 1873, and sang to the Senate his own songs, including "Let us all be unhappy on Sunday."

Building of this period includes Queen's Gardens, and the Episcopal church of St Andrew at the foot of it (1869), and the Victorian Gothic Hope Park Church for the United Presbyterians (1865). The first "kist o' whistles" (i.e., organ) in a St Andrews Presbyterian church was installed at St Mary's in 1874, amid violent controversy, such as greeted also the first weekday Christmas service in the Toun Kirk, in 1872. Old scandals got a new breath of life in 1873 when the demolition of an old public-house at the north-east corner of Church Street revealed a child's skeleton beneath a hearthstone. In Archbishop Sharp's lifetime somebody published a book about him in which Sharp was said to have lodged in a St Andrews change-house, before becoming a Regent in the university, and to have gotten with child one Isobel Lindsay, under promise of marriage, she being the innkeeper's sister-in-law. Sharp was said to have strangled the subsequent child and buried it beneath the hearth-stone. When he was Archbishop Isobel Lindsay stood up in the kirk and denounced him, more than once: for which the Provost personally put on her the "branks," or scold's bridle, still to be seen; and Sharp made her stand, thus bridled, at the Tron. But such old tales did little to moderate the goodwill of Victorian St Andrews to the first resident bishop of the Episcopalian diocese for a century and a half, Charles Wordsworth, a nephew of the poet. He is best remembered as founder of the Oxford and Cambridge Boat Race, and he also played cricket for Oxford. In 1853 he became Bishop of St Andrews, Dunkeld, and Dunblane, and from 1876 lived in the city, where he was invited to dine with the Presbytery, and even to preach in the Toun Kirk, in the spirit that has since been termed "ecumenical." A further departure from the Andrew Melville tradition was the institution of a Christmas party for the old folks, in 1879, by Bailie McIntosh, father of the pioneer marine biologist W. C. McIntosh.

When St Leonard's School started in 1877, the university itself had only 130 students; but attempts were being made to promote it with modern publicity methods, largely organized by William Knight, Professor of Moral Philosophy (1876-1903). A Chair of Education was founded, and degrees of Bachelor and Doctor of Science introduced, and a curious diploma titled *L.L.A.*, usually thought to mean "Lady Literate in Arts." It was granted to women successful in examinations held up and down the island, and overseas; and proved widely popular. Meantime a public-spirited Dundee lady, Mary Ann Baxter of Balgavies, was promoting the idea of a university college in Dundee, an old city which had recently expanded vastly in population through the boom in jute-manufacturing.

She gave £120,000 to found University College, Dundee, which started teaching in 1883. Her hope was that others would give generously, as had happened with university colleges in England, where, if one magnate gave £100,000, his rival would put down £150,000. Not so the Dundonians. Other local plutocrats said, "Well, if the Baxters want a college, let the Baxters pay for it." And, it is said, the other Baxters thought to themselves, "One fool in a family is enough." So Dundee did not grow as rich as Manchester; but still it was richer than St Andrews; and once again academic pundits here and there were saying, Why not suppress St Andrews, and distribute its endowments, such as they are? In the end money talked, most unexpectedly: for St Andrews received a windfall of £100,000 in 1889, from Australia. Alexander Berry, a former student, when emigrating to Australia, had been shipwrecked. His shipmates were eaten by cannibals; as he was too thin, the cannibals fed him on frogs in the hope of fattening him up; but before he was fat enough he was rescued, and lived long enough to gather a lot of wealth. Knowing his wishes, his surviving brother David sent along £100,000, a great sum in 1889. Quite apart from this windfall, the university had been generating some new energy in competition with its new rival across the Tay.

In 1882 W. C. McIntosh, Professor of Natural History (1882-1916), started work in an improvised laboratory consisting of a timber fever-hospital by the East Sands. In 1896 he was provided with the Gatty Marine Laboratory, through the generosity of an Englishman, Dr C. H. Gatty, and much valuable work was done for fisheries. St Andrews still had about a hundred fishermen with fourteen boats in mid-Victorian times. McIntosh was born in 1838, the year when the small medieval red gown was lengthened and sleeved to make a student's cloak. He died in 1931. Even in his nineties he was to be seen working at the Gatty, wearing his old red gown, and sometimes with his feet in a hay-box to keep them warm. His successor, Sir D'Arcy Wentworth Thompson, went to Dundee as professor in 1884, aged twenty-four, and held the Chair of Natural History at St Andrews from 1917 to 1948, when he died, having been sixty-four years a professor. Best known for his epoch-making book *Growth and Form*, D'Arcy had the widest-ranging of interests, and wrote, *inter alia*, glossaries of ancient Greek birds and fishes. When a hoopoe was shot on the golf-course in autumn 1930, D'Arcy took it about, wrapped in a silk handkerchief, and discoursed to his classes on Aristophanes' *Birds*. At graduations, when Principal Irvine made false quantities in his Latin, D'Arcy could be heard making strange whoops and whistles from behind his majestic beard, a beard the prickliness of which was attested by pretty bejantines with whom he danced in the 1930s, when he was in his seventies.

The principalship of the Aberdonian Classical scholar Sir James Donaldson (1886-1915) saw the university attaining a respectable position among the older universities. The Universities (Scotland) Act of 1889 had given increased powers to the University Court, a mainly non-academic body set up by the Act of 1858. For example, the Court could now institute new departments, with lectureships in default of professorships, and could appoint assistants, who had hitherto been privately hired by professors as they thought fit. A parliamentary annual grant of £6,300 was made, which in 1892 became £10,800. In 1892, also, Andrew Carnegie's Trust for the Scottish Universities was set up, which lent money to students for their tuition fees. In the same year women were admitted as graduating students. Then, too, the third Marquis of Bute was elected Rector, and served from 1895 for a second term. A wealthy and polyglot papalist peer, Bute was eager to make Blairs College, an Aberdeen seminary for priests, form part of the university of St Andrews; but the Vatican finally came down against him on this. Bute was also hostile to the affiliation of University College, Dundee, to the university, which had taken place in a half-baked fashion in 1890. Others for various reasons agreed with him, and, after wrangling and litigation, the union was dissolved in 1895, only to be re-made in 1897. In 1898, a Conjoint Medical School was established. Bute's munificence allowed the construction of fine buildings for natural sciences at St Andrews, and the inception of a Chair of Anatomy (1900). The Chandos Chair was specialized for physiology (1908), and it became common for intending medicoes to do their pre-clinical courses in old-world St Andrews before going to Dundee for their clinical years. Bute also donated largely for the extension of the Students' Union, which in 1892 secured the old house west of the College Tower, part of which is traditionally associated with the Admirable Crichton. In 1889 the brightest of undergraduate periodicals, *College Echoes*, began its career; and the Nineties produced that delightful Scots-American poet, Robert Fuller Murray, of *The Scarlet Gown*, and the *Scottish Student Song-book*, largely promoted by the Andreapolitan enthusiast Millar Patrick.

In 1897 a separate Science Faculty was instituted; and around that time chemistry flourished under Professor Purdie, whose opulent aunt, Mrs Purdie of Castlecliff, gave fine laboratories, which he extended. There was a good deal of private money about St Andrews up till the Kaiser's War of 1914, and some dozens of wealthy people built fine houses in the

138

western suburbs. During what was called "the Great South African War" imperialistic jingoism was in fashion, and an effigy of the Boer President Kruger was driven round the town to be burnt at the site of the old Mercat Cross, near the fountain in memory of the local novelist George Whyte Melville, killed in a hunting accident in 1878. Till the 1930s it was traditional to fling the President of the Union into it on Raisin Monday, the day when first-year students pay to their senior man or woman a pound of raisins, as fee for moral tutelage, and receive a Latin receipt specifying "*unam libram uvarum siccarum.*" On the same site a Covenanting mob had battered to pieces the coach of Archbishop Spottiswoode, after driving it round the streets with the burgh hangman inside.

The millionaire philanthropist Andrew Carnegie, a native of Dunfermline in West Fife, served as Rector from 1902 to 1908, and gave a fine sports park. In this connection the tongue of scandal tells how Principal Donaldson pulled a fast one. St Leonard's College had owned lands in the western suburbs, which in 1747 had passed to the United College, and were now vested in the University Court. Donaldson got Carnegie to sign a large cheque to enable the University to buy a tract that it already owned. When Carnegie said it seemed a high price, Donaldson replied that wealthy Dundee men were buying land for villas. Again, Carnegie wrote a cheque to build a modern indoor swimming-pool for the students. The Regius Professor of Mathematics, Sir Peter Scott-Lang, whose appointment had been a Tory political job in 1879, insisted on spending the money on an armoury for the cadet corps. When Carnegie asked to see his new swimming pool, Donaldson escorted him to the armoury door, and then the resourceful Coutts, the janitor, suddenly found he had mislaid the key; and they took Carnegie off to tea in University Hall, the women's residence built in 1896. Coutts the janitor was a power in those days. Percy Theodore Herring, who died in 1967, told how he applied for the Chair of Physiology in 1908 and put on his top hat and frock coat for the interview. When he reached the Hebdomadar's Room he saw a rival candidate with a short jacket and bowler hat. Coutts looked at them both, and showed in Herring to see Principal Donaldson, with the remark: "Here's the gentleman for the physiology chair. Ye'll no be wantin' tae see the ither man." On taking possession of his lab., Herring found only about two test-tubes, and complained to the Principal. "Och," said Donaldson, looking down again at his Byzantine history tome, "go and see Coutts about it."

In spite of a certain academic roguery here and there, and some insouciance, the Donaldson régime marked a new high point, and at the quingenary celebrations in 1911 for the university's foundation the staff included many men of world-wide distinction then or later, such as D'Arcy Thompson and Patrick Geddes, John Burnet in Greek and W. M. Lindsay in Humanity, A. E. Taylor and G. F. Stout, R. K. Hannay and J. D. Mackie and W. L. Lorimer, and the future Principal Sir James Irvine (1921-52), a distinguished chemist who proved a capable promoter and administrator. A surviving participant in the 1911 celebrations remembers one incident most vividly: at the chief banquet Hermann Diels, historian of Greek philosophy, launched out into a very long speech, during which the waiters, who were all German, stopped serving and drank so much that their locomotion was impeded. The lecturer in German, Dr Georg Schaafs, started swearing at them, but was overwhelmed by a relevant vocabulary more copious and sustained than his own. The quingenary service was held in the Toun Kirk, beautifully rebuilt in 1910 by Macgregor Chalmers. The generation before the 1914-18 War was characterized by somewhat ostentatious living by the small class with secure private incomes from investment, some scores of whom dwelt in St Andrews, with large domestic staffs to cater for their creature comforts. At the other end of Fife was a large coalfield, where the miners were notably militant, headed by Miss Jennie Lee's grandfather, Michael Lee, who won the Eight Hour Day campaign. His campaign song was: "Eight hours' work, eight hours' play, eight hours' sleep, and eight bob a day"—making forty-eight shillings for a six-day week. In one of their agitations, in 1912, the West Fife miners sent a squad of muscular colliers, equipped with stout sticks, to go round the mansions of the St Andrews *rentiers* and ask for contributions to the strike fund. The comfortable denizens of Hepburn Gardens and elsewhere mostly handed over some golden sovereigns, rather than risk having their lawns dug up at night or their conservatories bombarded with stones. Andrew Lang had been living largely in St Andrews since 1891, and was growing old. The advent of the miners terrified him. He buried all his coined gold in the garden, and fled to Banchory on Deeside, where he succumbed to a heart-attack. His wife testified, "It was really the strikes that killed him." It is said that nobody ever found his hidden cash.

During most of the 1914-18 war, in which 185 men of St Andrews were killed, the Principal was Sir John Herkless, formerly Professor of Church History. He was succeeded in 1921 by Sir James Colquhoun Irvine, whose work on the chemistry of sugars had been highly valued. One of his ambitions was to develop residences for men students, and he started with Chattan House, at the east end of Abbotsford Crescent, in 1921. Largely filled with ex-Servicemen, it proved hard to discipline. In 1927 Irvine secured a benefaction of £100,000 from an American Scot, Dr E. S. Harkness, with which he built a much larger residence for men, St Salvator's Hall, facing the castle (1930). Meantime the university had been dubiously embellished by the Younger Graduation Hall (1929), an eclectic structure by Paul Waterhouse, whose signature appears at the east end of the south front, the letters *P* and *W* above and below a Noah's Ark on stylized waves. Waterhouse also completed All Saints' Church (1924), an Episcopalian "High" Church, containing now the best modern sculpture in the city, a Virgin and Child by Hew Lorimer of Kellie Castle. The Martyrs' Kirk was rebuilt in 1927, with a more imposing crowstepped outline, not long before the reunion of the main Presbyterian bodies in 1929. The College Kirk was refurbished internally, with the addition of a stone screen between ante-chapel and nave, by Reginald Fairlie (1930). St Leonard's Chapel was restored in 1952 by Sir David Russell, in memory of a son killed in the war, Ian Lindsay being architect. There are some fine modern stained-glass creations in various St Andrews kirks now, by Douglas Strachan, Lewis Davis, William Wilson, and others: the best organ is that of the Toun Kirk as reconstructed in 1966. It has also a fine peal of fifteen bells (1926).

In 1926 Principal Irvine allowed the revival of the Kate Kennedy procession. This student pageant started as a "rag" in the quadrangle in the 1840s, became a scurrilous and riotous public demonstration, and was finally suppressed after Saturday, 5 March, 1881, when a specially outrageous display coincided with a heavy snowstorm and a nautical disaster. The three-master *Merlin*, of Sunderland, struck on the rocks at the Witches' Lake. A rope was thrown out to the crew of eight, who raised a cheer. A moment later, the ship slid off the reef, and all eight, in their stiff yellow waterproofs, drowned within sight of a thousand spectators on the fifty-foot cliffs. The Kate Kennedy procession, each April, includes the heroic Divinity student, John Honey, who in 1800 rescued, single-handed, seven men from a wreck in the East Bay. As a memorial to him, it is said, the students started their walk from the College Kirk to the pierhead after Sunday services. Another student who died untimely was the poet Robert Fergusson (1750-74), whose work in the Scots tongue inspired Robert Burns, who used his first royalties to erect a headstone on Fergusson's grave in Edinburgh's Canongate kirkyard. He too walks in the Kate Kennedy procession, with the French revolutionary Jean Paul Marat, who bought his MD from St Andrews, as did such unlikely alumni as Edward

Jenner, the champion of vaccination against smallpox, and Dr Bowdler, who made Shakespeare fit reading for the Victorian family circle.

Principal Irvine also revived, in 1927, the "Regenting" system, as a type of moral tutorship of undergraduates: since when St Andrews has become rather noted among Scottish headmasters for its familial pastoral care of volatile youth. During the 1930s that remarkable literary partnership, Edwin and Willa Muir, made their home in the town; and Edwin used to walk daily over the Links, meditating his imaginative poems, a very different reaction to the historic greensward from that manifested by the novelist Anthony Trollope. While staying at Strathtyrum in 1868 with the publisher John Blackwood, Trollope tried his hand at the Gowf, and his resultant vociferations were heard all over the Elysian Fields at the fourteenth hole. After a particularly atrocious stroke, he fainted with grief and collapsed upon the turf. Even to the greatest golfers of this century, to be sure, the Old Course has sometimes proved troublesome.

The 1920s and 1930s saw the growth of a "New Town" south of the Kinness burn, mainly of housing schemes undertaken by the municipality, a leading figure of the time being Provost Norman Boase, who also was influential in reconciling the Town and the R & A, bodies which had for decades been at loggerheads. A group of enthusiasts between the wars founded the St Andrews Preservation Trust, to protect and restore the rich and varied heritage of houses from the sixteenth century on. Another enthusiast, Mr A. B. Paterson, himself a playwright, took the lead in converting an old cow-house into the lively Byre Theatre, which seats about seventy persons and has done dramatic wonders on a shoe-string budget. Theatrical activity has been somewhat discontinuous in St Andrews since John Knox graced with his presence a play the happy ending of which was the hanging of a papalist garrison-commander. In 1939 two major dramatic events occurred: Hitler invaded Poland, and the Royal and Ancient Golf Club admitted professionals for the first time. At that period the university had about eleven hundred students, some five hundred of them in Dundee, and about two-fifths of them women. Of the young ladies at St Andrews a high proportion were English, often from higher income-brackets than their Scots partners in student dances and ensuing romances, which added to the social comedy of the town—a comedy, by the way, not yet exploited by a novelist. Not in many Scottish burghs could one ever have heard a church-going lady remark, "It is such a set-off to the service to have the lessons read by a Baronet." Before 1939, though English girls were frequent, an English male student was rarer than a Negro; and indeed the most conspicuous outlanders were American Jewish medicals, many of whom were splendid pugilists, and put St Andrews ahead in Scottish inter-university boxing matches. But after 1945 Englishmen began to invade the place in great numbers, St Andrews having for some years a "priority" in the pecking order next to Oxford and Cambridge. This was in part a reflection of the fact that Scotland had relatively many universities compared with England in 1945; and, to be sure, many of the men from English schools were ancestrally Scotsmen, sons of Scots physicians and bureaucrats and executives engaged in "spoiling the Egyptians." One result of the new pressure on university places was a re-opening of the problem of the relations between University College, Dundee, and the University of St Andrews, with which it had been partially united in 1897. After extensive argument and a Royal Commission, a more thorough unification was enacted, the academic activities benorth the Tay being grouped in Queen's College, Dundee, incorporating University College, the Conjoint Medical School, and the Dundee School of Economics. The Principal appointed in 1953 to run the unitary scheme was Sir Malcolm Knox, a painstaking administrator with a devotion to Hegelian philosophy and vintage clarets. After he had conscientiously carried out the government's intentions for a decade, rationalizing activities to avoid needless duplication in each college, the government policy switched, and it was decided, for political window-dressing, to set up a separate University of Dundee, which came to pass in 1966. Scotland's senior university thus lost, with much else, its clinical medical school, one of the finest in the United Kingdom. To secure clinical teaching for the pre-clinical students, St Andrews asked Dundee for a block booking of places, but this proved to be impracticable. The University of Manchester in England promptly made a block-booking: so that St Andrews medicals will henceforth emerge with the M.B., Ch.B. of Manchester, an institution well placed for clinical material.

In the 1950s the target of the unitary university was 3,400 undergraduates, half in Queen's College, Dundee, and half in St Andrews. For the 1970s Dundee aims at about 6,000, and St Andrews at 4,000, which will still leave it a relatively small and intimate university. The historic city is still small and intimate also, with some 8,500 permanent residents. There is no university city in Europe so truly dominated by its university as St Andrews—not Uppsala or Heidelberg, Urbino or Poitiers. More than a quarter of the earned incomes in St Andrews depend directly on the university. Undergraduates from the big cities usually relish the privilege of studying in a seaside holiday resort without bustle or vulgarity, and with fine opportunities for the well-balanced life. Some have been known to come primarily for the Old Course, of which Peter Thomson, multiple winner of the World Open Championship, declared in 1955, "It is the best course in the world, and there is none like it. I am the more convinced of that the more I play it." Other students like the possibilities of pottering about in small boats, which have multiplied around the harbour as the full-time professional fishing-boats have shrunk to a half-dozen. Others fancy the championship tennis courts, or the excellent hill and shore lands for cross-country running. Those who ski bless the belated erection of a Tay road bridge giving swift access to snowy tracts of the Highlands; and more culture-loving types find the Forth road bridge handy for popping up to shows in Edinburgh. If any student has a taste for undergraduate curricula or post-graduate research there are lots of first-class offerings, and there will be more as plans develop, whether the inquirer's mind runs on low temperature physics or the higher textual criticism of the New Testament, philosophy or Classics or Romance philology, history or astronomy or marine biology, or all sorts of other specialist studies undreamt of by Bishop Wardlaw, the pious founder, and far off St Kenny in his hermitage and the ready-handed Pictish High King Angus. There are now some five million Scots in Scotland, but it has been estimated that there are twenty million people overseas who claim Scots ancestry and have some interest in their ancestral homeland. Among those from this Scottish *Diaspora* who have been benefactors of St Andrews in the past one thinks especially of Andrew Carnegie and Edward Stephen Harkness. One American Scot, Dr Russell Kirk, fell so much in love with St Andrews that he wrote a delightful book about it. It may be that, as air travel becomes commoner, expatriate Scots in Texas or Ontario or New South Wales will increasingly send their young hopefuls to take undergraduate or post-graduate courses in Scotland's oldest university, to realize the ideal set up by Principal Steven Watson, on taking office in 1966, that of making St Andrews, *par excellence*, "Scotland's International University."

From *Scotland*

Cassel, 1971, Chapter 1.
A succinct summing-up of the Scottish character.

ANOTHER HISTORIAN, Gordon Donaldson, notes "the existence of a critical and independent spirit as an important feature of Scottish church life and indeed of the Scottish character." A certain missionary zeal has often been evinced by Scots, and even before Protestantism the European learned wrote of the "very fervent nature of the Scots," *praefervidum ingenium Scotorum*. But there could be a Jekyll-and-Hyde syndrome about Scottish religion too, with plenty of hypocrisy of the "Holy Willie" sort. In Burns's time the mass Communions in which several parishes combined, such as he portrayed in *The Holy Fair*, had a mixture of the austere and the Rabelaisian, the devotional and the Bacchanalian, that could hardly be paralleled outside the ancient Greek cults of Dionysos.

As to the ability of the ordinary Scot to thrive when transplanted, Daniel Defoe noted, nearly three centuries ago, that "so many more of the Scots servants [*employees*] which go over to Virginia settle and thrive there . . . that if it goes on for many years more, Virginia may be rather called a Scots than an English plantation." In 1888, in his book *Greater Britain*, Sir Charles Dilke observed: "In British settlements, from Canada to Ceylon, from Dunedin to Bombay, for every Englishman that you meet who has worked himself up to wealth from small beginnings without external aid, you find ten Scotchmen." An English historian of the Scottish people's social development from 1560 to 1830, Dr T. C. Smout, draws attention to the evidence that in 1521 the Scottish peasantry could be called "elegant" compared with those of France; they tried to rival the lesser nobles in their dress and arms, "and if one of these should strike them they return the blow on the spot." This democratic spirit of "Jock is as guid as his maister" has been a recurrent theme down the generations. As also the egalitarianism of "We're aa Jock Tamson's bairns."

One factor that has made the Scots "a peculiar people" is the Covenanting phase of the seventeenth century, when the mass was somewhat made over in the image of the Old Testament Jews, a nation that had made a Covenant with God Almighty. The subtle text-disputing authoritarianism and its countervailing fissiparous sectarianism have kept breaking out ever since that period of reckless idealism and feckless fiasco. Indeed, they are largely responsible for the specific aboulia, lack of willpower, and disseminated sclerosis of the Scottish nation today.

Many more bouquets and brickbats could be added to those assembled in the foregoing pages; but perhaps the sample data collated will introduce to the reader the typical Scot as a schizophrenic creature at once realistic and recklessly sentimental, scientific and soldierly, bibulous and kilted, teetotal and trousered, diligent, religious, liberal, warm-hearted, poetry-loving, devoted to law, learning, and mercantile enterprise, friendly, unassuming, living graciously, supine, dirty, fond of closing public houses unseasonably, violent and drunken, and addicted to casual homicide, too careful with money, generous, rash, disputatious, shy, loquacious, aggressive, refined, humane, zealous, hypocritical, adaptable, democratic, equalitarian, and peculiarly related to the Almighty.

From *Aeschylus: The Oresteia*

University of Oklahoma Press © 1974, "translated into English verse from a scientifically conservative Greek text."

This was his last work, posthumously published. The extract, from the Agamemnon, lines 1372-1559, illustrates the logaoedic sprung rhythm which allows for flexibility and literalness in the translation at the same time.

(*The* CHORUS LEADER *breaks off his sentence as the palace doors are opened, and* CLYTEMNESTRA *is seen, standing over a silver-sided bathtub, with the corpse of* AGAMEMNON *wrapped in a robe with animal designs, and the corpse of* CASSANDRA.)

CLYTEMNESTRA

Till now I have made many time-serving speeches:
henceforth I shall not be ashamed to state the contrary.
For, plotting hostile acts against a foe
pretending friendship, how could one set the nets
of injury so high he could not leap out?
    This struggle of mine, long premeditated,
starting from an ancient quarrel, has been fought at last.
I stand where I struck the blows, with the deeds done.
I acted in such a way—I shall not deny it—
that he could not escape nor ward off his doom.
    An endless wrap-around, like a fishing net,
I fix about him, an evil wealth of cloth,
and I strike him twice. In the space of a couple of groans
his limbs went slack. And there, as he lay fallen,
I hit him a third time—three is a lucky number—
in thanks for a vow to Death, the saviour of—corpses!
    Thus fallen, he gasps his soul away in rushes;
and blowing forth a sharp wound of blood
he hits me with a dark shower of crimson dew,
while I rejoiced, as a crop grows bright with rain
that comes to swell the grain growing in the corn ear.
    All this being so, My Lords of the Privy Council,
you could rejoice if you would, but I am boasting.
Were it fitting to pour reproaches over a corpse,
them one might justly pour, and more than justly.

147

Such a bowl of cursed evils he mixed for the family
and now has come home and himself drunk it off.

CHORUS LEADER

We are amazed at the audacity of your speech,
uttering a boast like this about your husband.

CLYTEMNESTRA

You test me out, as an irresponsible wife.
But with unflinching heart I declare—and you know it—
it is all the same whether you approve or censure—
this is Agamemnon, my husband, and my corpse,
a product of the work of this right hand of mine,
a craftsman that makes things even. That is how it is.

CHORUS   *Strophe 1*

Ah, lady, what virulent poison
have you eaten, some earth-reared edible,
or a poison sprung from the wrinkled brine,
to bring on yourself this sacrifice
and the curses the people utter?
You threw him down; you butchered him. You will be banished,
an object of mighty hate to the citizens.

CLYTEMNESTRA

You sentence me to banishment from the country,
with the citizens' hate and the curses the people utter,
though you passed no such sentence against this man here,
when, heeding it no more than the doom of a sheep,
with plenty of sheep among his well-fleeced flocks,
he sacrificed his own daughter, my dearest child,
by way of a charm against the winds of Thrace.
Surely you ought to have banished him from the land,
as penalty for pollution? Yet when you hear
of my actions you pass a heavy sentence.
     Realize, when you threaten, that I am ready to accept
the rule of the winner in a fair and equal fight.
If a god fulfil the contrary, you shall learn,
by a lesson late in life, what sound sense is.

148

How grandly you plan your ambition!
And how subtly you speak! How arrogantly!
But your mind is crazed by the deeds of blood;
the bloodshot glitter that shines so clear on your eyes
is a sign of madness.
Yet, even so, bereft of friends, you shall be punished
and pay for a wound, a wound as a penalty.

CLYTEMNESTRA

This too I declare to you and duly swear it:
I swear by the perfect Justice of my daughter,
by the Ruin and the Fury to whom I sacrificed him,
that no foreboding of fear enters my house
so long as fire is kindled on my hearth
by Aegisthus, loyal to me still, as in the past.
For in him we have a strong shield of confidence.
Here lies the man who outraged me as a wife,
the darling of every golden girl round Troy.
And the prisoner of war here, the watcher for omens,
who shared his bed, the teller of prophecies,
his trusty concubine, a filthy whore
of the lower decks. . . . But the pair are not without honour:
he lies in a robe of state; and she, like a swan,
having sung her last lament at the point of death,
lies lovingly beside him. The robe of my pride
brought me this tasty fish too from his spawning bed.

CHORUS *Strophe 2*

Oh, oh! I pray for a fate that would swiftly,
with no long sickness, painlessly visit us,
bringing among us all here the sleep
that lasts forever and knows no waking,
now that our kind and much-enduring guardian
has been brought low for a woman's sake,
and by the hands of a woman he perished.

Oh, criminal Helen, breaking the law,
you alone destroyed the many,
the countless souls slain at Troy;
and finally now you adorned yourself
with long-remembered clamour for unpurged bloodshed.
Truly there was then in the house
an irresistible Strife, a husband's woe.

CLYTEMNESTRA

Do not pray for a fate of death,
through grieving at this;
and do not turn your anger on Helen
as a murderess, the sole destroyer of many
souls of the men of Greece
and causer of pain incurable.

CHORUS   *Antistrophe 2*

O Demon, ever haunting this palace
and our two kings descended from Tantalus,
now you are wielding, to my distress,
a power equal in soul through women,
Helen and Clytemnestra. She is standing
like a dread raven above his corpse
and boasts her chanting is righteous and lawful.

CLYTEMNESTRA

Now you have got correct the judgment you pronounce,
when you summon the thrice-fatted
Demon of this family.
For from him a blood-licking lust
swims and flows and grows—before the old ache ceases,
fresh festering pus.

CHORUS   *Strophe 3*

ruly, mighty and heavy in wrath
for Pelops' house is the Demon you speak of.
Woe, woe, what an evil plague
of a ruinous fortune, insatiable!

Woe, woe, by the will of Zeus,
causer of all, worker of all.
For what is done for mortals on earth without Zeus?
Of all this is there anything not wrought by gods?

Refrain 2

O my king, my king,
how shall I weep for you?
From my loving heart what shall I say?
You lie in this web like a spider's,
having breathed your life away in an impious death—
Oh, woe is me!—on a lowly couch, ignobly,
brought down by a treacherous doom, by a wife's hand
with a two-edged weapon.

CLYTEMNESTRA

You are asserting that I did this deed.
Do not even think that I
am the consort of King Agamemnon.
For, taking the form of the dead man's wife,
the ancient cruel Spirit exacting vengeance
for Atreus, that harsh banqueter,
paid this man out, and sacrificed
a perfect full-grown victim for Thyestes' children.

CHORUS   *Antistrophe 3*

Who will testify, taking an oath,
that you are free from the guilt of this murder?
How so? But perhaps you had
as accomplice his father's punisher.
Now, forcing his way through blood,
pouring in streams shed by the kin,
the swarthy god of Slaughter is dealing justice
to those children devoured, and their chill clotted gore.

Refrain 2

O my king, my king,
how shall I weep for you?
From my loving heart what shall I say?

151

You lie in this web like a spider's,
having breathed your life away in an impious death—
Oh, woe is me!—on a lowly couch, ignobly,
brought down by a treacherous doom, by a wife's hand
with a two-edged weapon.

CLYTEMNESTRA

Not ignoble, to my thinking,
was the death that this man died.
And, as for treachery, did not he
by treachery cause ruinous loss for the family?
My child, and his, whom I reared and mourn for, Iphigenia,
he treated unjustly, and justly he suffers.
In Hades' house let him not boast,
having paid for what he started
with a death caused by a sword.

CHORUS *Strophe 4*

I know not where to turn, bereft
of reason's resourceful thoughts,
as the Pelopid dynasty crumbles and falls.
I dread the thunder rain that tumbles the house
in blood and ruins. For now the small drops cease,
and Fate is sharpening Justice on other whetstones
to cause another act of damage.

Refrain 3

O earth, would you had buried me first,
before I saw him laid so low,
here in a silver-sided bathtub!
Who will bury him? Who will mourn him?
Truly will you have the heart to do this,
to bewail your husband after slaying him
and perform unjustly for his soul
a favour that is no favour, in return for mighty deeds?
Who at his tomb, sending forth with tears
a eulogy of the marvellous man,
will labour in truthfulness of mind?

152

CLYTEMNESTRA

It is no concern of yours
to trouble about this matter. By our hands
he fell, he died, and we shall bury him,
not with shedding of tears by the household.
But Iphigenia, his daughter,
welcoming as is proper,
will go to meet her father
at the swift ferry of Charon on the river of woes,
and put an arm about him and kiss him.

A Bibliography

WE ARE very much indebted to Miss E. B. S. Robertson, M.A., of the University Library, St Andrews, for permission to publish a preliminary list of Douglas Young's writings on which she is at present at work. It covers his books and pamphlets, and his contributions to periodicals on Classical subjects only. The others, mainly on Scottish topics, are voluminous and a complete list of these will ultimately be published in *The Bibliotheck*. Miss Robertson meanwhile wishes gratefully to acknowledge the help she has received in her research from Professor Robert Carnie of Calgary University, and from her colleague at St Andrews, Mr Kenneth J. Fraser. Copies of all his writings will in due course be available for consultation in the National Library of Scotland which has acquired his papers.

A CHRONOLOGICAL CHECKLIST

BOOKS AND PAMPHLETS

1940-1 *The Auld Aiberdeen Courant and neo-Caledonian Spasmodical: a political and literary gallimaufray*. Edited by D. Young.
  [Typescript periodical. 3 issues at irregular intervals all published.]

[1942] *The free-minded Scot: trial and defence of Douglas Young*. Glasgow, The Caledonian Press.
  [Report of trial of DY before Sheriff Norman Macdonald in Glasgow Sheriff Court, 13 April 1942.]

1942 *Quislings in Scotland*. Glasgow, Scottish Secretariat.

1942 *A Scot's free fight*. Glasgow, Scottish Secretariat.

1943 *Auntran blads: an outwale o verses*. (Poetry Scotland Series No. 1). Glasgow, Maclellan.

1943 *Fascism for the Highlands? Gauleiter for Wales?* Glasgow, Scottish National Party.

[1943] *William Wallace and this war*. Speech at the Elderslie Commemoration 1943. Glasgow, Scottish Secretariat.

1944 *An appeal to Scots honour. A vindication of the right of the Scottish people to freedom. The unheard appeal. Edinburgh High Court 1944, with Douglas Young's petitions from prison*. Glasgow, Scottish Secretariat.

1944 *British invasion of Scottish rights . . . why industrial conscription and delegated legislation are unconstitutional in Scotland*. Glasgow, Scottish Secretariat.

1946 *The re-colonisation of Scotland, a broadcast address*. Glasgow, Scottish Secretariat.

155

1947   *A braird o thristles: Scots poems.* (Poetry Scotland). Glasgow, Maclellan.

[1947]   *International importance of Scottish Nationalism.* Glasgow, Scottish Secretariat.

1947   *"Plastic Scots" and the Scottish literary tradition.* Glasgow, Maclellan.

1947   *Saltire modern poets series.* Ed. by D. Young with M. Lindsay. Edinburgh, Oliver and Boyd.

1948   *Idea of a Scottish National Congress: a plea for a functional approach to Scottish control of Scottish affairs.* Edinburgh, Douglas Young.
[St Andrew's Day address under the auspices of the Scottish Convention in the Iona Community House, Glasgow, Tuesday, 30 November 1948.]

1949   *Labour record on Scotland, 1945-1949.* An address . . . to the Scottish Universities Labour Party, Aberdeen Branch on Thursday, 16 December 1948. Glasgow, Scottish Secretariat.

1949   *The use of Scots for prose, being the John Galt Lecture for 1949.* (Papers of the Greenock Philosophical Society). Greenock, Greenock Philosophical Society.

1950   *Chasing an ancient Greek: discursive reminiscences of a European journey.* London, Hollis & Carter.

1950   *Selected poems* (The Saltire modern poets). Edinburgh, Oliver & Boyd for The Saltire Society.

1952   "The making of a poet: some notes on Fergusson's educational background." In *Robert Fergusson 1750-1774: essays by various hands to commemorate the bicentenary of his birth,* edited by S. G. Smith. London, Nelson.

1952   *Scottish verse, 1851-1951; selected for the general reader by Douglas Young.* London, Nelson.

1955   "A note on Scottish Gaelic poetry." In *Scottish poetry: a critical survey,* ed. by J. Kinsley. London, Cassell.

1955   "Scottish poetry in the later nineteenth century." In *Scottish poetry: a critical survey,* ed. by J. Kinsley. London, Cassell.

1955   "The Scottish student today." In *The Scottish companion,* ed. by R. Spence· Edinburgh, Richard Paterson.

1955   *The Treaty of Union between Scotland and England, 1707: the legal basis of the United Kingdom of Great Britain.* With some constitutional considerations excerpted by Douglas Young from recent writing on the treaty. Glasgow, Scottish Secretariat.

1956   *Romanisation in Scotland: an essay in perspective.* Tayport, Douglas Young.
[Revised and enlarged edition of an address given to the Dumfriesshire and Galloway Natural History and Antiquarian Society, 26 March 1954. Read also at Abertay Society, 11 November 1954.]

1957   *The Puddocks: a verse play in Scots frae the auld Greek o Aristophanes.* Tayport, Douglas Young.
    1958   *The Puddocks: a verse play in Scots from the Greek of Aristophanes.* 2nd edition with glossary and additional notes. Tayport, Douglas Young.

1957   "Scotland's story." (*Scotland's Magazine Annual,* 1957). Text written by Douglas Young. Edinburgh, *Scotland's Magazine.*

1959   *The Burdies: a comedy in Scots verse by Aristophanes and Douglas Young.* Tayport, Douglas Young.
    1966   *The Burdies: a comedy in Scots verse by Aristophanes and Douglas Young.* Revised edition for official Festival production at the Edinburgh International Festival.

1961   *Theognis. Ps.-Pythagoras. Ps.-Phocylides. Chares. Anonymi Aulodia. Fragmentum teliambicum. Post E. Diehl.* edidit Douglas Young. (Bibliotheca Teubneriana). Leipzig, Teubner.
    1971   Iterum edidit Douglas Young. (Bibliotheca Teubneriana). Leipzig, Teubner.

1962   "The nationalism of Hugh MacDiarmid." In *Hugh MacDiarmid: a festschrift* ed. by K. D. Duval and S. G. Smith. Edinburgh, Duval.

1964   "Borrowings and self-adaptations in Theognis" (*Miscellanea Critica, I*). Leipzig, Teubner.

1965   *Edinburgh in the age of Sir Walter Scott* (Centers of Civilization Series, 17). Norman, University of Oklahoma Press.

1966   *Scots burds and Edinburgh reviewers: a case study in theatre critics and their contradictions in regard to the first International Festival production by Edinburgh's Royal Lyceum Theatre Company, 1966 compiled by Douglas Young.* Edinburgh, M. Macdonald.

1967   *Edinburgh in the age of reason: a commemoration by D. Young, A. J. Youngson, G. E. Davie, D. Forbes, Lord Cameron, A. Fraser.* Introduction by Douglas Young. Edinburgh, Edinburgh U.P.

1968   *Venus with a vengeance: the* Hippolytus *of Euripides in English verse by Douglas Young.* Hamilton, Ontario, printed for the Department of Classics, McMaster University.

1969   *St Andrews: town and gown, royal and ancient.* London, Cassell.

1970   "A sketch history of Scottish Nationalism." In *The Scottish Debate*, ed. by N. MacCormick. London, Oxford University Press.

1971   *Scotland.* London, Cassell.

1974   *Aeschylus. The Oresteia. Translated into English verse from a scientifically conservative Greek text by Douglas Young.* Norman, University of Oklahoma Press.

CONTRIBUTIONS TO PERIODICALS ON CLASSICAL SUBJECTS

1955   "Author's variants and interpretations in Frithegod." *Archivum Latinitatis Medii Aevi (Bulletin du Cange)*, XXV, 71-98.

1955   "The extent and degree of Romanisation in Scotland." *Trans. Dumfriesshire and Galloway Nat. Hist. and Antiq. Soc.*, 3rd ser.

1955   "On Planudes' edition of Theognis and a neglected apograph of the *Anthologia Planudea.*" *La Parola del Passato*, X, 197-214.

1959   "Miltonic Light on Professor Denys Page's Homeric theory." *Greece and Rome*, 2nd ser., VI, 96-108.

1964   "Gentler Medicines in the *Agamemnon.*" *Classical Quarterly*, NS, XVI, 1-23.

1964   "The Greeks' colour sense." *Review of the Society for Hellenic Travel*, IV, 42-45.

1964   "Some types of error in manuscripts of Aeschylus' *Oresteia.*" *Greek Roman and Byzantine Studies*, V, 85-99.

1965   "Some puzzles about Minoan woolgathering." *Kadmos*, IV, 111-112.

1965   "Some types of scribal error in manuscripts of Pindar." *Greek Roman and Byzantine Studies*, VI, 247-273.

1966   "Notes on the text of Pindar." *Greek Roman and Byzantine Studies*, VII, 5-22.

1967   "Never blotted a line? Formula and Premeditation in Homer and Hesiod." *Arion*, VI, 279-324.

1968   "Author's variants in the manuscript tradition of Longus." *Proceedings of the Cambridge Philological Society*, No. 194, NS 14, 65-74.

1969   "Minoan woolgathering: a rejoinder." *Kadmos*, VIII, 39-42.

1971   "Readings in Aeschylus' *Choephoroe* and *Eumenides.*" *Greek Roman and Byzantine Studies*, 12, 303-330.

1971   "Second thoughts on Longus's second thoughts." *Proceedings of the Cambridge Philological Society*, 197, 99-107.

1972   "Readings in Aeschylus' Byzantine Triad." *Greek Roman and Byzantine Studies*, 13, 5-38.

LIST OF SUBSCRIBERS

The Douglas Young Memorial Volume Fund gratefully acknowledges the subscriptions of the following:

Prof. J. W. L. Adams
R. H. Armstrong
Miss M. R. Baxter
Mrs B. Beaton
Prof. W. Beattie
Dr E. K. Borthwick
The late W. Oliver Brown
George Bruce
The late Mrs J. R. Calder
R. G. Cant
D. F. Collins
A. Y. Cooper
Mary, Countess of Crawford
    and Balcarres
The late Miss H. B. Cruickshank
Dr J. Davies
Miss Lavinia Derwent
The Hon. Mrs C. Drummond
Miss N. V. Dunbar
Dundee University Library
K. D. Duval
East Lothian County Council
    Edinburgh Public
Libraries
Baroness Elliot of Harwood
Dr A. W. F. Erskine
Prof. R. E. Fantham
Mrs M. Y. Glendinning
I. C. Gordon-Campbell
Dr C. M. Grieve
Prof. P. L. Heath
Prof. A. S. Henry

International P.E.N. Club English
    Centre
International P.E.N. Club Scottish
    Centre
Mrs I. J. Jack
President J. F. Leddy
Dr R. A. Lillie
The late Dr Eric Linklater
    and Mrs Linklater
R. S. Little
Miss M. C. Lochhead
Miss Alison Lowe
Dr Gordon Lowe
Prof. and Mrs K. G. Lowe
D. MacArthur
Mr and Mrs J. McCallum
I. H. MacDonald
The late Rev. J. and Mrs
    MacKechnie
R. O. MacKenna
Somhairle Maclean
McMaster University Department
    of Classics
D. S. MacPhail
Prof. and Mrs J. MacQueen
Dr E. A. Marshall
Mrs Naomi Mitchison
Sir Iain Moncreiffe of Moncreiffe
Mrs M. Muir
Mr and Mrs D. Murison
M. le Comte V. de Pange
Mrs M. S. Rae

Mrs A. J. J. Ratcliff
Miss N. E. Ratcliff
Rev. D. C. and Mrs Read
Mrs Margaret Ritchie
Lord Robertson
Miss E. B. S. Robertson
Prof. Giles Robertson
R. H. S. Robertson
Dr J. Russell
"Scotsoun" per Dr G. Philp
The late G. Scott-Moncrieff
Prof. H. Seton-Watson
Dr D. Sider
Prof. O. Skutsch
The late Sydney Goodsir Smith

Prof. P. A. Stadter
Dr M. A. Stewart
Stirling University Library
R. G. Sutherland
Miss R. D'A. Thompson
Prof. E. G. Turner
Dr and Mrs Heinz Valtin
Prof. F. Watson
Dr D. E. R. Watt
Miss Clara Young
Mrs Douglas Young
J. S. Young
Mrs Mila D. Young
Miss Yana Young

We should also like to thank the people who have subscribed to the Douglas Young Memorial Fund for a microfilm collection to be kept at the Department of Greek, St Andrews.